This book sheds light on an almost unknown military campaign conducted by a French army, 100,000 men strong. The army was referred to by the French king as the 'Sons of St. Louis' and was pitted against parts of the regular Spanish army and a numerous militia. The cause of the war was a revolution in Spain in 1820 which brought in a 'Liberal' government and the Spanish parliament, the Cortes, held Ferdinand, the Spanish king, a virtual prisoner. Ferdinand appealed for help from the French who were supported by an army of Spanish Royalists. A few years earlier many of these Royalist volunteers had been France's bitter enemies and had fought Napoleon's generals to a standstill.

The French troops who crossed the Pyrenees were part of a newly-forged army, taken from the debris of Napoleon's old regiments augmented with newly-raised conscripts and many inexperienced officers drawn from émigrés and the old nobility who had returned to France after the Battle of Waterloo. However, it was led by battle-hardened former Imperial officers and was placed under the overall command of the king of France's nephew, who was also in line for the throne of France.

Since 1824, when a small number of works appeared in France, there has been no readily available book on the subject, in any language.

A full account of the campaign is given, together with detailed descriptions of the armies of France and Spain, illustrated with contemporary pictures and modern interpretations and including maps and plans of the war. The final and crucial battle, the taking of the forts on the island of the Trocadero, opposite Cadiz, is given special attention. Although small by recent European standards, the fight was decisive for bringing about the end to the war and for establishing the spirit of the new French Royal army and restoring France to a position as one of the leading world powers.

The organisation of the armies and the uniforms of the post-Napoleonic French and Spanish forces are covered in detail. The critical book list adds to the reader's understanding of the sources used.

Ralph Weaver has made a life-long study of military history, particularly of Europe in the 19th century. He began his military career with the Sealed Knot before giving up the sword for the pen. He has been the editor of the journal of the Continental Wars Society for the past 25 years and has written and illustrated books and magazine articles on military history. He trained as a land surveyor in the Civil Service and has used his map-making skills in battlefield walking and table top war gaming. He has been collecting books, pictures, photographs and reference material on uniforms with a view to writing a definitive history on the subject. As well as conducting research on military topics, his latest interests include cooking and looking after grandchildren.

THE HUNDRED THOUSAND SONS OF ST LOUIS

The French Campaign in Spain
April to October 1823

Ralph Weaver

Helion & Company

Helion & Company Limited
26 Willow Road
Solihull
West Midlands
B91 1UE
England
Tel. 0121 705 3393
Fax 0121 711 4075
Email: info@helion.co.uk
Website: www.helion.co.uk
Twitter: @helionbooks
Visit our blog http://blog.helion.co.uk/

Published by Helion & Company 2018
Designed and typeset by Mach 3 Solutions Ltd (www.mach3solutions.co.uk)
Cover designed by Paul Hewitt, Battlefield Design (www.battlefield-design.co.uk)
Printed by Lightning Source Limited, Milton Keynes, Buckinghamshire

ISBN 978-1-912174-09-6

British Library Cataloguing-in-Publication Data.
A catalogue record for this book is available from the British Library.

For details of other military history titles published by Helion & Company
Limited contact the above address, or visit our website: http://www.helion.co.uk

We always welcome receiving book proposals from prospective authors.

Contents

List of Illustrations

Preface

This book owes its origin to the research undertaken to support a display put on at the Salute Wargames Show. The information gathered seemed to fill more and more notebooks, albeit electronic ones, that only a small proportion could ever be displayed and it seemed churlish to waste it. Much of it was barely known to modern writers in the English language and even in France the subject remains a backwater in military history. Spain in the 19th century was convulsed by interminable civil wars and revolutions so that the republican experiment begun by an obscure battalion officer in 1820 gets little mention.

The French campaign in Spain in 1823 was not 'a campaign' in the strict sense of the word, but several, sometimes disjointed and uncoordinated, campaigns going on at the same time. For this reason the book is set out geographically rather than chronologically, although each section is treated in the order the events occurred.

The name of the most significant battle, on the island of the Trocadero has become well known to Parisians and tourists as a fashionable meeting spot. The London Trocadero as a place of amusement was copied from the French original. In 1826 a military parade was held in Paris on the area now known as the Trocadero and a re-enactment of the capture of the Spanish fortifications was included. To add realism to the display a full-size model of the fort, constructed from cardboard, formed the centrepiece.

Introduction

This book sheds light on an almost unknown military campaign conducted by a French army, 100,000 men strong. This army was referred to by the French king as the 'Sons of St. Louis' and was pitted against parts of the regular Spanish army and a number of national guards, militia and volunteers. In 1820 a revolution in Spain established a 'Liberal' government and the Spanish parliament, the Cortes, held Ferdinand, the Spanish king, a virtual prisoner. Ferdinand appealed for help from the French who were supported in the field by Spanish royalists and numerous guerrilla bands that had already taken up arms against the liberal authorities. A few years earlier many of these troops had been France's bitter enemies and had fought Napoleon's generals to a standstill.

The New French Army

The French troops who crossed the Pyrenees were part of a newly forged army, taken from the debris of Napoleon's last regiments with newly raised conscripts and many inexperienced officers drawn from émigrés and the old nobility who had returned to France after the battle of Waterloo. However, there were still many senior field officers; battle hardened former Imperial generals though placed under the overall command of the king of France's nephew. Some, at least, of the NCOs and rank and file were also old soldiers who knew their business and provided a level of 'seasoning' to the young soldiers who had not shared their experiences during the Empire. After Waterloo and the occupation of France by the Allies the new French army of Departmental Legions had been raised from volunteers, conscription was only brought in when the Allies departed with the indemnity demanded from the French government.

The Spanish Constitution

During the turmoil of the Peninsula War, French armies ravaged Spain and government was largely in the hands of local committees, the king, Ferdinand, being a prisoner in France. In 1810 one of these committees based in Cadiz attempted to form a national government and a number of leading politicians drew up a constitution. Most of those gathered in Cadiz were 'liberal' minded, with representatives

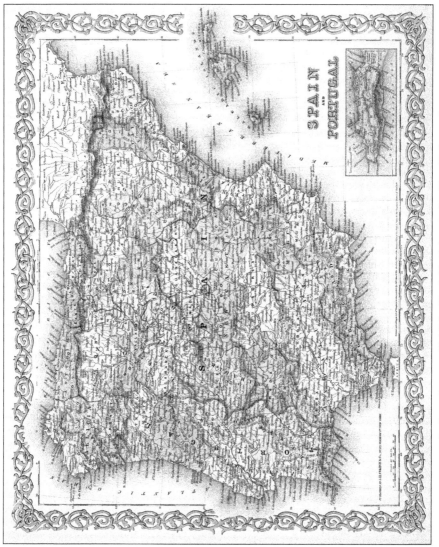

Spain main map. (Published by J. H. Colton & Co, New York, 1855)

from the Catholic Church and the old nobility in the minority. The constitution was not revolutionary on the French model, but was biased towards the liberal minded and progressive elements of the population. Spain had long been an absolute monarchy ruled by a branch of the Bourbon family, supported by the Catholic Church and the privileged nobility, but the new constitution swept away this medieval system and brought in the concept of a monarchy which could reign, but not rule (much like the then current system in Great Britain). Power would rest with the parliament, the Cortes, and ministers would be accountable to members of that body. This became known as the 'Constitution of 1812' and was the principle plank of the Liberal government from 1820 to 1823.

Court dress of a member of the Cortes.
(Delineations of the most remarkable costumes of the different provinces of Spain and also of the military uniforms, bull fights, national dances, etc. of the Spaniards. London: Henry Stokes, 1823)

While the constitution was welcomed by many Spaniards, it was hated by the old rulers, including the king and also the peasants, who stood to gain little by it and were in thrall to their local priests and aristocracy and genuinely felt a deep loyalty to the royal house. The seeds of conflict were thus cast, between those liberals who supported the constitution and opposed by the king, the conservative aristocracy and the majority of the population.

Spain's attempt at a more liberal government (and indeed Portugal's whose revolution took place at the same time) did not go unnoticed elsewhere. In the address to the Senate and House of Representatives of the United States of America made by President James Monroe on 3 December 1822, reference is made to the hope that Spain will find peace and good government. This message to the American elected representatives is better known for its promulgation of the doctrine of the sanctity of the New World against the meddling from the Old.

Tactics used on the battlefield in 1823

The campaign fought across the Spanish peninsula highlights the way tactics laid down in the field manuals were applied in the actual fighting. Many of the sources, particularly the French, are quite detailed in their descriptions of what took place, eye witness accounts and diaries particularly. So called 'official histories' (and this applies to most wars) speak grandly of advances of corps, of divisions, of brigades, or even regiments, when much of the fighting was conducted at company level. Most early 19th century armies had similar regulations, as they fought with similar weapons which dictated what ranges were effective and, for example, how the troops were to be arranged, distances between lines and how many paces the officers were to be stationed in front of the men. It was not until rifled weapons were introduced on a large scale and the adoption of breechloaders in the latter part of the century that tactics had to be changed to suit the new circumstances.

Infantry companies generally formed in three lines with the third line coming forward to form a skirmish group in front of the first line. This line was made up of the better marksmen and sometimes would have different weapons from the rest of the company (more sophisticated sights, for example). After the skirmish line had achieved some success in disrupting the cohesion of the enemy facing them, by concentrating their fire on enemy officers and NCOs, standard bearers and signallers, the second two lines would form a column, advance and, in theory, the enemy would not stand, but retreat or break. (If they did not then the advancing unit would stand and the firefight continue until one side showed signs of wavering). Reading the accounts it is clear that the elite companies in a battalion, the voltigeurs and grenadiers, would invariably lead any attack, with the fusilier companies, in column, following to complete the victory. The French Light battalions were considered as shock troops and were frequently selected to open an engagement, the voltigeur and carabineer companies, the elite of the elite, leading. A regimental diary reports that one Light Infantry regiment commenced the campaign with over 1,100 men and six months later was reduced to little more than 400 effectives. For major actions, such as the storming of the Trocadero fortifications, companies of voltigeurs and grenadiers from several battalions were grouped together to form the head of the attack, with the fusiliers following once a successful breach had been made. At the taking of Logrono, the assault was entrusted to the voltigeur company of the 20th of the Line.

What follows from this is that few troops actually did any fighting. Where large numbers of casualties are reported and acknowledged, it is most likely that one side lost cohesion and were routed, with the casualties inflicted in the subsequent pursuit. Hence records show the losing side admitting to killed, wounded and 'missing' (prisoners). The victors rarely refer to any of their troops as missing. There are exceptions of course, where troops are involved in street fighting or defending buildings where they cannot retreat or run.

Battle reports suggest that the Spanish regular regiments followed similar tactical regulations; one account speaks of a Spanish light infantry battalion forming a line of battle opposite a French battalion and trading volleys.

Strangely, artillery was not particularly effective in Spain, due to the nature of the topography. In one battle in the mountains, the French brought two batteries to support their infantry, but had to be left behind as the road they were using just petered out. Where artillery was used more effectively was in the numerous sieges conducted by the French. They had to bring the heavy guns from the artillery depots in France as they were not part of the field army. Even so they were content to blockade many Spanish strongpoints using the artillery to destroy the defences, or at least make a practicable breach rather than risk major casualties in a direct assault.

Cavalry also was used sparingly, some mounted actions described in regimental histories involved less than a hundred men on each side. Cavalry was useful in scouting and occupying or denying positions to the enemy. As with the infantry, the cavalry were rarely deployed by regiment, squadrons or even troops were used for most purposes. One attack noted was undertaken by the escort of a French general, barely 20 men. A French cavalry regiment rarely consisted of more than 400 men. There are always exceptions and at Logrono two squadrons of light cavalry charged through the town gate and cleared the streets, but had to leave house to house fighting to the following infantry.

Names

In some accounts the names of the Spanish towns referred to in the official records will not be found on modern maps. This is because names have changed, or altered their spelling in the nearly 200 years since the events described. In such cases I have given both the name given in the battle reports and the modern name so that the action will be intelligible to the reader who is following the campaign with an up-to-date map in front of them.

A word on casualty figures and numbers of troops

As the Spanish constitutional authorities were swept away following their defeat, little has remained of any official records and few of the participants wrote memoirs in what would have been a politically awkward situation. The years following were disturbed by the Carlist Wars and by the time the country was stable, all the participants were long gone. The Spanish Royalists had little government machinery and had no interest in recording their enemy's dispositions, other than wildly exaggerated claims when they achieved some victory. The French, of course, wrote copiously on the war glorifying the exploits of the new Royalist army fighting under the White Flag of the Bourbons. They, according to their own accounts, inflicted massive losses on the Spanish constitutionalists while suffering little or no losses themselves! A contemporary American journal quoting reports from a European paper, comments sarcastically as follows:

> Mina, seven weeks ago, had 700 men under his command. With these 700 men he made a precipitate flight. Out of these 700 men 8,000 deserted. In his flight, Mina attacks Vich with 4,000 men, where he loses half his forces by desertion, and 2,600 in killed and wounded. How many remained? Ballesteros was abandoned by all his troops except three incorrigible constitutionalists. He divides

his three constitutionalists into several parties. These parties are attacked by the detachments of Molitor's division and out of three constitutionalists; Ballesteros loses 1,700 (and retires at the head of ten thousand men). Abisbal, before his defection, had 1,500 men; his defection lessened this number at least one third. Zayas collected the remains of Abisbal's 1,500 men and it is with these remains we find him on the road to Seville, commanding 5000.

With these exaggerations and the propaganda from all sides, trying to find what losses were inflicted during the fighting is almost impossible. With the number of men changing sides, deserting and actually killed and wounded, reliable figures cannot be found. Admittedly, at the taking of Logrono the French claimed to have killed 30 of the defenders, which seems almost reasonable, only to spoil it by saying they suffered no casualties themselves. Another source does tell us that an officer who led a cavalry squadron later died of his wounds.

Bearing this in mind, I have quoted army strengths and casualties for many of the engagements described in this book, these having been taken from the various sources, mainly French of course, and may or may not reflect the actual losses incurred. The total number of 'enemy' casualties quoted in the French sources exceeds the strength of all the Spanish armies at the start of the campaign, which clearly shows that these reports should be treated with caution, or that they are propaganda pure and simple.

Sources

The list of books quoted in the bibliography looks to be quite comprehensive, but a word of warning: many of the French works, especially those written at the time had a political agenda. This was to show the loyalty of the army and navy to the cause of the reinstated Bourbon monarchy, which at the time was not thought to be a forgone conclusion. As noted above, the new army was a mixture of inexperienced young recruits, veterans from the Empire who owed their ranks and preferment to Napoleon and many members of the aristocracy who had either fought against the Imperial armies, or had waited in exile for better days. Accounts of the war appear in a number of works, but a careful inspection shows that often the same words and phrases appear in many of them. Almost as if one 'official' view of the war was prepared which was then copied by all the others. Newspapers devoted many column inches to descriptions of battles with much blood and gore to satisfy the most ardent reader, which may have been intended more to sell papers than report the truth!

1

The Spanish Revolution

Why, on the morning of 7 April 1823, did a small group of men dressed in French Imperial Guard uniforms, waving the red, white and blue tricolour flags, stand on the southern bank of the Bidasoa River and shout defiance at a larger group of Frenchmen who displayed the white standard strewn with gold *fleur de lis* of the reigning Bourbon monarchy of France?

The river, rising 40 miles away high up in the Pyrenees mountains, here formed the frontier between France and Spain. The river's name came from the Basque language with the Basque country extending far beyond either side of the river itself. It flowed between the foothills and down into the Bay of Biscay. The ex-guardsmen were political refugees from France who had taken refuge in Spain after the battle of Waterloo and the final abdication of Napoleon. The Frenchmen on the north bank of the river were part of a larger force assembled to carry out the policy of the alliance of sovereigns who were pledged to maintain the reactionary status quo in Europe after the upheavals of the French revolution and Napoleonic wars. The political aim of this overwhelming power was to restore the king of Spain, Ferdinand VII, to his previous position as absolute ruler of the Spanish nation and empire.

Napoleon's armies had spent several years attempting to subdue the Iberian Peninsula, without success. They had forced Ferdinand from his throne and replaced him with Napoleon's brother, Joseph, but by 1814, supported by British troops and money and the overwhelming efforts of the Spanish people, Ferdinand was reinstated. However, during his absence, a group of Spanish politicians of liberal views (for that time) formed a committee or junta and introduced a new constitution for the country. In essence it was that the king would act as a figurehead for the state but that the real power would lie with the Spanish parliament, the Cortes. This, the 'Constitution of 1812' was initially accepted by Ferdinand on his return to Spain after the expulsion of Napoleon's troops. However as the concept of a constitutional monarchy was anathema to Ferdinand he soon began to contrive ways to restore the absolute monarchy of the pre-Napoleonic period.

Decrees were issued in 1814 deposing Liberal ministers, re-establishing religious houses and restoring the Inquisition! Supporters of Joseph Bonaparte and the former French administration were banished from Spain. Many liberal minded people and

French Foot artillery, General Vallin orders the artillery to open fire on the French liberals across the Bidasoa. (Unknown artist)

A casualty on the first day of the campaign, a 'liberal' in French uniform on the banks on the Bidasoa, Clerjon de Champagny. (Open source)

Map of northern Spain, extract from Spain main map.
(Published by J. H. Colton & Co, New York, 1855)

especially lower ranking army officers looked upon this return to the despotic old ways with fear.

Events in continental Spain during the Napoleonic wars had led to a degree of home government in the Spanish colonies in South and Central America. Support for Ferdinand had been quite marked, but only as a reaction against the French and the governing bodies of the American colonies had declared their independence from King Joseph. They also opened trading relations with Britain and broke many links with Spain. With the return of Ferdinand and his absolutist policies they were loath to give up their newly established independence. Spain had some troops in the Americas, but these had struggled to re-establish colonial control. The fight for independence led by competent military commanders such as Simon Bolivar and José de San Martin, was all but accomplished by the time that Ferdinand decided to send an expedition to bring the wayward colonies back into Spain's (economic and political) sphere. Admittedly some parts of the New World remained loyal to the Spanish Empire, New Spain (Mexico and the central Americas), Florida, Cuba, and Peru.

After the end of the wars in Europe in 1815, the Spanish government determined to re-establish their authority over their American empire. An army of 10,000 men under General Pablo Morillo was formed at Cadiz and sailed to South America. However, despite some local successes, and the seeming pacification of Venezuela the forces of Morillo were never strong enough to achieve their aim, although he did enter into discussions with the revolutionary general, Simon Bolivar. In 1819

Ferdinand VII, King of Spain 1808 to 1833.
(Goya)

a second expedition was fitted out to send to South America to restore Spanish sovereignty. Troops were again assembled around the port of Cadiz under the Spanish commander-in-chief, Don Henry O'Donnell, Count of Abisbal. No ships were then available to transport them as the Spanish navy was in a very poor state, so the government bought five 74-gun ships of the line from Russia! The ships lasted barely five years in Spanish service before they were broken up. As the army was about to leave European shores an epidemic of yellow fever broke out which forced the authorities to disperse the battalions as a safety measure to stop the spread of the disease. At this time O'Donnell's loyalties to the king were suspect as his name had been linked to an anti-Ferdinand conspiracy and he was replaced by the Count de Calderon, a successful general who had fought in Mexico and was a former Viceroy of New Spain.

January 1820

The army at Cadiz consisted of 16,000 men, including a small force of cavalry, a brigade of artillery, the infantry regiments of Rey; Principe; Princess; America; España; Seville; Asturias; Valencia; Aragon; Canaries; Guadalaxara; Cordoba; Cataluna and Corona and a corps of sappers and miners.

An uprising against the king and in favour of the Cortes and Constitution was brewing among some of the officers of the Cadiz army and the imminence of its departure for America persuaded them to bring the date of the insurrection forward. On the first day of January 1820, the commander of the 2nd battalion of the regiment of Asturias, Lieutenant-Colonel Don Raphael Riego, formed up his men, gave them a rousing speech declaring the sovereignty of the Constitution of 1812 and the Cortes and marched out to raise other disaffected units of the army.

The revolution had its origins in the period of the Napoleonic Wars where the Spanish government was hopelessly divided between the French backed regimes in Madrid and wherever French armies occupied territory, Spanish local

Riego portrait.
(Unknown contemporary artist)

Spanish Army during the 1820 revolution. (Unknown artist)

government where the guerrilla forces operated and where British and Spanish regular troops were in control. By 1814 Spain, with the aid of Allied (British and Portuguese) armies was free of the French and the king, Ferdinand, was back in the capital.

Before the French intervention, Spain had a system of government based on the absolute power of the king and his advisors and a vast number of 'officials' who owed their preferment to royal patronage, and enjoyed privileges whether they performed a useful function or not. This was the system that Ferdinand and his supporters strove to re-establish. They had strong support from the mass of the Spanish people, who, influenced by the Catholic Church, were intensely loyal to the monarchy. However Ferdinand faced, what turned out to be, insurmountable difficulties. After six years of war the government coffers were empty. And the loss of the American colonies cut off the revenue they had formerly supplied.

The threat of another revolt by his exasperated subjects in 1820 forced Ferdinand to once again sign up to the 1812 Constitution, but now the liberal supporters of the Constitution had formed into two camps, the 'moderates' and the 'extremists'. The moderates believed in the right of the king to reign (if not to rule) and the extremists cared little even for the concept of monarchy. There was more than just ideology between the two factions, it seems that personality also played a part; the two sides actively disliked each other. The fact that many of the extremists in the military had worked their way up the promotion ladder by their own efforts, rather than royal patronage may also have added further venom to the mix. During the Napoleonic war the army had existed on subsidies from Great Britain, but after 1815 these had ceased, so the king was left with no alternative but to cut down the size of the army, many officers of liberal views faced being relieved of their positions and therefore their incomes and prestige. The depression that followed from the end of the war and the loss of the American markets meant taxes no longer met expenditure; the only remedy at the time seemed to be to print more money. This led eventually to a downward spiral as the cash became worth less and less, eventually selling at a discount of 80 percent.

This brought about, on 1 January 1820, Riego's launching of the revolution. He found, in the areas where his battalion marched, little enthusiasm for his ideas; indeed many of his own men deserted the cause. Desperate times called for desperate measures and when he arrived in Algeciras on 1 February he made a general order abolishing the tithe all peasants had to pay the church, the state tobacco monopoly and a reduction of 50 percent in general taxes. Malaga, on the Costa del Sol, now declared for the revolution and three weeks later so did La Coruna in the far north, followed by Saragossa and Barcelona (always a revolutionary city).

The king, thoroughly alarmed by the turn of events agreed to again sign up to the 1812 Constitution, although he worked to thwart most of its aims. The seeds of disaster were soon cast; the revolutionaries while accepting the constitution would not accept the new liberal minded government. The new Cortes met in July 1820 and was immediately faced with the same problems the king's ministers had faced before them; they had no money to carry out their program. One of their first acts was to propose the dissolution of part of the revolutionary army, which was acting under

Riego's orders. The government was in a desperate position, ministers appointed by the king could not get the Cortes to work with them and many members of the Cortes were handing out favours to friends, just as the old corrupt royal politicians had done. Open violence broke out in July in Madrid when the Royal Guard revolted and was put down by Riego and the National Guard.

The Spanish public wanted economic recovery and a stable currency and they got neither, so when the French army marched into Spain in April 1823 they were looked upon as liberators rather than invaders. Some Constitutionalists fought well against the French, but had to contend with a lack of support from among their fellow revolutionaries and a rising tide of royalist guerrilla activity in the countryside as well as better organised royalist regiments fighting alongside the French.

Spanish peasants who had spent years fighting the French, under the twin banners of 'Altar' and 'Crown' could make little sense of the principles of the Constitution, as their local priests gave it no support and saw no benefit in joining a movement which had little sympathy for the authority of the Catholic Church and most peasants knew no other form of government than that of royal despotism. Local resistance to the Cortes began to grow and some towns and districts refused to obey its pronouncements, guided by the clergy and by their landlords and the nobility. From small disorganised bands to a regular field army the Royalist forces became to be known as 'The Army of the Faith', described as such by themselves and the French. Thus Riego and the Constitutional government had to face apathy from a large part of the population and outright antagonism from another part. Surprisingly the Cortes managed to maintain support from a large part of the regular army, considerable numbers of National Militia and provided fixed garrisons in a number of towns and cities throughout Spain. As the crisis deepened supplies and military stores were dispatched to many of the Constitutional garrisons, strengthening their resolve, as the French found to their cost during the campaign of 1823.

The Spanish Government had confidence that they could contain the Royalist forces and, as they controlled the body of the King, they held the advantage. They thought that any congress of European leaders would just be a talking shop and that little would come of it. At no time did they think that they would have to face a foreign army. Even Notes from foreign governments, delivered by their ambassadors in Madrid did not seem to shake their confidence. They saw the build-up of the French army on the frontier as just another form of pressure, even as the French prepared to move, they did not take the threat seriously. Bands of Royalists, defeated in the field, fled across the frontier, to be rearmed by the French and sent back again, seemed to be the only external threat that they would have to face.

What galvanised the French to make the move into Spain, when all their experience seemed to show that only disaster would ensue? The Congress of Verona authorised the French to act, but what really pushed them was the suggestion by Tsar Alexander of Russia to offer to send an army of 150,000 men to Germany and Western Europe to stop any undue revolutionary support for Spain while the French army was employed outside the country. After the fall of Napoleon, Alexander fancied that he was the man to decide the fate of Europe and preserve those absolute monarchies which governed most of the continent. Unfortunately, no one in Europe wanted that to happen and was about the only thing they could all agree on!

A meeting of the Spanish Cortes was held on 3 March 1823 when the subject of discussion was should the seat of government be moved because of the threat of French intervention. After some arguments, Seville was chosen; it was far from the French frontier and near to Cadiz which was looked upon the main stronghold of the Constitutional cause. It was one thing to pass a resolution, it was quite another to persuade Ferdinand to comply. He put off the journey claiming ill health, but on 20 March a cavalcade of coaches, escorted by a battalion of militia, set out from Madrid and by 10 April arrived in Seville. As the war progressed even Seville became unsafe, as far as the Cortes was concerned, and further plans were made to send him, a virtual prisoner, to the city of Cadiz, situated on a fortified island on the Atlantic coast. The government, made up of the most diehard Constitutionalists, also repaired to Cadiz.

So why did the revolution of 1820 fail? An observer of the social events of Europe, Karl Marx, sitting in the safety of the British Museum Reading Room, puts it quite simply. He writes, 'It was a middle class revolution, and more especially, a town revolution, while the country [people] ignorant, lazy and wedded to the pompous ceremonies of the church, remained passive observers of the party strife they did hardly understand …' Closer to home, General Morillo, who led one of the Constitutional armies in Galicia, north-western Spain, before giving up on the Cortes, wrote to the Duke of Angoulême:

> If the Cortes had sanctioned the bill on the seigniorial rights and thus despoiled the grandees in favour of the multitude, Your Highness would have encountered numerous, patriotic and formidable armies, which would have organised themselves, as they did in France, under similar circumstances.

There in a nutshell is the answer, a popular revolution which turned out not to be popular at all with the majority of the Spanish people and reliant on certain elements of the army and those members of Spanish society especially who were prepared to sign up for the militia who saw in the revolution their own best interests. There were, of course, idealists who sought to modernise Spain and dispense with its overseas empire and limit the influence of the king and the Catholic Church, but they could not carry the mass of the country people with them.

Many Spanish of liberal views, who had given the Cortes their support, were sought out after Ferdinand regained power and despite pleas for clemency by the French, suffered the extreme penalty. In a period of one month, August to September 1824, the Madrid official Gazette reported the death by shooting or hanging of 1,200 people. A few did manage to evade the executioner by taking ship, or making the dangerous journey overland, and headed for safer shores, some to England or America and surprisingly many found a welcome in France, no doubt under the watchful eyes of the police.

2

The French Army

Departmental Legions

With the second return of Louis XVIII after the 'Hundred Days' and the battle of Waterloo, one of the first acts of his government was to reorganise the army removing any 'imperial' influence, not just flags, badges and symbols but even the look of the army itself. The regimental system was abolished to be replaced with regionally based Departmental Legions. The new Legions took their titles from the district where they were raised and stationed and consisted of two battalions of infantry, each of eight companies of 71 men, a chasseur battalion also of eight companies, but each consisting of only 47 men, a troop of 48 mounted scouts and a company of light artillery of eight guns. As there was a shortage of horses, most of which had been taken by the cavalry regiments, the troops of the Legion's mounted scouts existed mostly on paper.

The infantry of the new Legions wore a white uniform, of a similar cut to the former imperial uniform, with various combinations of coloured collars, lapels, piping, cuffs and cuff flaps. The Legions were arranged into groups of 10, with facings in royal blue; yellow; scarlet; pink; crimson; orange; sky blue; green and madder red. The first five of the group had yellow metal buttons, the second group, white metal. The chasseur battalions had green uniforms. While this satisfied the political aspirations of the royal government it was disastrous from an efficient military point of view. A report presented to the Minister of War stated that the desertion rate amongst the locally recruited battalions was unacceptably high, that many units did not speak French, but rather their local language (Basque, Breton, Provencal) or dialect and that there was little if any co-operation between Legions. The legions had to rely on volunteers, as the conscription had been banned by the Allies following the victory at Waterloo, companies and battalions were woefully under strength and few of the prescribed mounted scouts even had any horses! The report recommended that the only way to remedy these defects was that the regimental system be re-established.

The Royal Guard

The return of the Bourbons in 1815 was the occasion of the disbandment of Napoleon's Imperial Guard and the raising of a new Royal Guard. Not essentially new though as most of the units had existed before the revolution. The guard had six companies of mounted Bodyguards to the King; a company of Royal Bodyguard artillery with 14 guns; a company of Royal Gendarmes; one company of Royal Guard Light Horse; two companies of (mounted) Musketiers; two companies of mounted guards to the king's brother (*Garde-du-Corps de Monsieur*); one company each of mounted Grenadiers; Guards of the Door; Hundred Swiss and the Guards of the Palace (*Gardes de la Prevote de l'Hotel du Roi*). One regiment of six battalions of French Guards; one regiment of four battalions of Swiss Guards; one company of artillery for each of the French and Swiss regiments; a corps of Marshals and a section of military engineers. The total for the Royal guard was just under 12,000 troops with 4,700 horses. The cost of this establishment was enormous and beyond the reach of even the king of France's pocket.

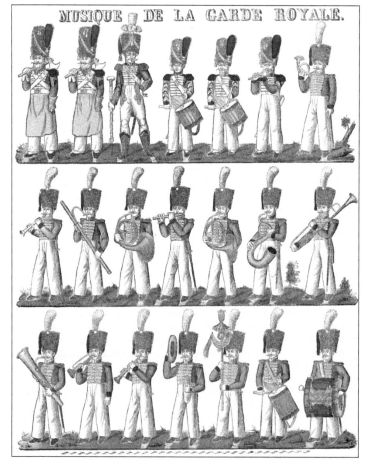

French Guards band, sheet of paper soldiers, Epinal print. (Open source)

Swiss Guard being reviewed by its Colonel General, the infant Duke de Bordeaux, later the legitimist pretender to the French throne as 'Henry V'. (Author's collection)

By 1823 the French army had a reformed Royal Guard of the sovereign's personal guards and a corps of infantry and cavalry and gendarmerie. The king was escorted by a company of Royal Bodyguards on foot, where all the guardsmen were of officer rank. In 1817 this guard amounted to 333 men, reduced to 255 by 1821. There were now only four companies of mounted bodyguards, also of officer rank. The mounted companies were named after their colonels, Harvé (the commander of the senior company of the French royal bodyguards who were the successor of the former Scotch Guards of the French kings); Gramont; Noailles and Luxembourg. These household troops were ranked one grade above similar ranks in the line troops. There was also a mounted unit of the 'Bodyguards of Monsieur', the title referring to the younger brother of King Louis XVIII, as the next in line to the throne. He succeeded Louis on his death in 1824 as Charles X.

The Royal Guard infantry was made up of eight regiments of Foot Guards, the first six recruited from French citizens and the 7th and 8th from among the Catholic Swiss cantons, which also had an additional identification, the 1st and 2nd Swiss regiments. The Guard cavalry also had eight regiments, the 1st and 2nd Mounted Grenadiers, the 1st and 2nd Cuirassiers, one regiment each of Dragoons, Mounted Chasseurs, Lancers (the only regiment so named in the French army, there were no lancer regiments in the Line) and Hussars. The Artillery had one each of a Foot and a Mounted regiment and an Artillery Train. The personnel of the artillery totalled 1,200 men and the material consisted of 24 field guns, 12 howitzers, 100 wagons of all descriptions and required 600 horses. The Royal Gendarmerie, a militarised police force, had an elite company for service around the royal residences, 24 'legions' for service in the provinces and a special gendarmerie for the city of Paris.

The Foot Guards were recruited from soldiers of the former Imperial Guard and men supplied by the Departments of good health between the ages of 19 to 27 and former soldiers below the age of 30. At the same time a number of older former guardsmen, officers and NCOs who were over 50 were retired from service. In 1818 the Royal Guard was opened to volunteers who could afford to buy their own uniforms. They served a fixed term of eight years. The regiments of Guards were organised into two divisions, each of two brigades. The 1st and 4th Regiments in the 1st brigade; the 2nd and 5th in the 2nd brigade and the 3rd and 6th in the 3rd brigade. The two Swiss regiments made up the 4th brigade. Each regiment of the guards had three battalions. The first and second battalions each had six fusilier companies and one each of elite companies of grenadiers and voltigeurs. The third battalion had six companies of chasseurs and one each of carabineers and voltigeurs as the elite companies.

Each regiment had a staff of 17 officers, including a colonel; a lieutenant-colonel; a major; three *chefs de bataillon*; and administration and medical officers. There was a 'small staff' of NCOs, including adjutants; the Drum-Major; three corporal drum-mers; senior sapper; music master and a band of 30 musicians and a number of master armourers, tailors and shoemakers.

The company was commanded by a *Capitaine Commandant* assisted by a second captain and four lieutenants of various grades. There was a sergeant-major, four sergeants, eight corporals and 98 men in the grenadier, carabineer and voltigeur companies and 108 men in the fusilier and chasseur companies. The grenadier and carabineer companies also had in addition two sappers.

The manual for NCOs of the Foot Guards laid down that the men were to wash and shave every day and were to be provided with hot water to do so. All NCOs and the NCOs and men of the 1st and 2nd Regiments were allowed to grow moustaches, no larger than the depth of the upper lip. No wax was allowed to be used. Sideboards could not be worn below the level of the earlobe and the hair was to be kept short. The men's feet were to be inspected every week. The bearskin headdress was to be kept in a waterproof cardboard box on the Bread Shelf when in barracks and was to be brushed once a week. The greatcoat was to be properly rolled into a sausage shape and strapped to the top of the pack in its blue and white striped cover. When on parade the cover was to have round cardboard ends, painted blue with the company device stencilled in the middle (ie, grenade, *fleur de lis*, hunting horn). The cross-belts were to worn over the greatcoat, except when on the march or on campaign when, to protect the equipment, the cross belts were worn underneath.

The cartridge pouch and its brass ornaments was to be polished to a high shine and when deemed satisfactory to be coated with two layers of lacquer. In the field it was to be covered with a sheet of black waxed linen. The cross-belts were whitened and also covered with a lacquer. Black leather shoes, sabre and bayonet scabbards were to be thoroughly waxed to preserve their waterproofing.

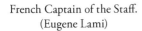

French Captain of the Staff.
(Eugene Lami)

On campaign the socket of the bayonet was to be covered with a waterproofed linen bag which was kept tight with a draw-string. This was to prevent any moisture getting into the scabbard. Scabbards were to be kept waxed to keep them waterproof. Sergeants had the responsibility to make sure that side arms were kept clean and rust free and well oiled. No doubt the troops of the Line were also subject to the same rigorous routine.

Those members of the guard who were past active service, but not decayed enough to be sent to *Les Invalides* were enrolled into the veterans companies, the *Compagnies Sedentaires*. There were 10 companies; the first named the Company of Veteran NCOs and the second the Company of Veteran Fusiliers. The members of these companies were selected for their record of good service and had to have served five years in a guard unit.

Infantry

A royal ordnance of 23 October 1820 abandoned the Departmental Legions and 60 regiments of infantry of the Line (properly termed just 'infantry', but used here and throughout this book, to distinguish between guards, infantry regiments and light infantry) and 20 regiments of light infantry replaced them. They would be identified by their newly allocated numbers. The new regiments were to have a staff and three battalions, but due to a shortage of men only the first 40 regiments had three battalions, the remainder only two, until such times as numbers allowed a full compliment. Each battalion consisted of eight companies, six fusilier, one grenadier and one voltigeur company. The light infantry regiments had two battalions with the centre companies termed chasseurs, the elite companies having the titles carabineers and voltigeurs. Each battalion was to have a compliment of three officers and 80 NCOs and men (one sergeant-major; four sergeants; a quartermaster corporal; eight corporals; two drummers or cornets and 64 men.) The regiments of three battalions should have consisted of 88 officers and 2,031 NCOs and men. Two battalion regiments were to have a complement of 62 officers and 1,359 NCOs and men. However, these were the ideal complements, many old soldiers retired from the service (as we shall see in a later chapter), volunteers were not forthcoming in sufficient numbers and with no conscription there was never enough new men to fill up the ranks, actual numbers were nearer 1320 NCOs and men for the three battalion regiments and 880 for the two battalion regiments. Each centre company also had a compliment of two *enfants de troupe*, historically children of NCOs whose family followed the regiment and were educated by the charge of the regiment. Children of officers had their own special schools.

A decree of 2 February 1823 created a third battalion to each of the two battalion regiments. A second decree, of the same date, created four further regiments of infantry, each of three battalions, numbered 61 to 64.

French Line infantry, 51st Regiment. (Post card by Pierre Albert Leroux)

In addition to the French regiments, there were a number of non-French units. Four regiments of men recruited from the Swiss cantons, mainly those of the French speaking and predominately Catholic cantons. They were not part of the French establishment and were numbered 1 to 4 on a separate list. Each regiment was composed of three battalions, each of six companies (one of grenadiers, four of fusiliers and one of voltigeurs) of 104 men and an artillery section of a lieutenant and 40 men. Including the staff of the battalion and the regiment, a total of 1,956 officers and men.

There was also a 'foreign' legion (made up of foreign soldiers who wished to continue service in the French army after Waterloo) entitled the Legion of Hohenlohe, which was on 22 February 1822 reorganised as the Regiment of Hohenlohe of three battalions, each of eight companies. The regimental commander, Prince Louis of Hohenlohe-Waldenburg-Bartenstein, was a German nobleman who had fought against Napoleon as a general in the Austrian army before taking a commission from Louis XVIII on Prince Louis's arrival in France. The colonel was a Patrick Murphy and a number of his fellow countrymen were enrolled as officers, John Dillon, Arthur Dickson, Thomas Brown and Richard Johnston. Among the list of officers other names belie their origin, Martinez, Molinari, Wetzlar, Zienkowitz and Herdt von Hutten.

There were small numbers of units in what remained of the French overseas colonies after they had lost most to England after the Napoleonic wars. A native unit in Pondicherry in India was manned by sepoys and was organised as a battalion of light infantry, complete with an elite company of carabineers. There were some companies in the West Indies of French soldiers and locally raised conscripts.

Cavalry

The cavalry of the line retained the distinction between heavy and light. The heavy cavalry was made up of two squadrons of *Carabiniers de Monsieur* (see above) and six regiments of cuirassiers. The remainder of the cavalry consisted of 10 regiments of dragoons; 24 regiments of mounted chasseurs and six regiments of hussars. The cuirassiers, as well as numbers, were also given 'royal' titles; the rest of the cavalry had regional titles. Orders of battle could refer to either the number of the regiment or its royal or regional title (or both).

Carabineers	du Monsieur
Cuirassiers	
1	de la Reine
2	Dauphin
3	d'Angoulême
4	de Berri
5	d'Orleans
6	de Condé

Dragoons
1	du Calvados
2	du Doubs
3	de la Garonne
4	de la Gironde
5	de l'Hérault
6	de la Loire
7	de la Manche
8	du Rhône
9	de la Saône
10	de la Seine

Chasseurs
1	de l'Allier
2	des Alpes
3	des Ardennes
4	de l'Arriege
5	du Cantal
6	de la Charente
7	de la Correze
8	de la Cote d'Dor
9	de la Dordogne
10	du Gard
11	de l'Isere
12	de la Marne
13	de la Meuse
14	du Morbihan
15	de l'Oise
16	de l'Orne
17	des Pyrenees
18	de la Sarthe
19	de la Somme
20	du Var
21	du Vaucluse
22	de la Vendee
23	de la Vienne
24	des Vosges

Hussars
1	du Jura
2	de la Meurthe
3	de la Moselle
4	du Nord
5	du Bas-Rhin
6	du Haut-Rhin

Cavalry regiments had a staff of 12 officers and 10 men, four squadrons each of eight officers and 132 NCOs and men, a total of 44 officers and 538 NCOs and troopers. In 1823 the strength of all the regiments of Chasseurs à Cheval were increased to six squadrons, the first and the sixth squadrons in each regiment were armed with lances. The squadron was the tactical unit and was commanded by a captain and comprised two 'divisions' each under a First Lieutenant, comprising two platoons under a Second Lieutenant, each of which had two sections, under a sergeant, each of two sub-sections with a corporal and alternately six or seven troopers. For the cavalry alone over 25,000 horses were required to be purchased and maintained. The distinction between the cavalry proper and the dragoons was continued as historically they had been raised as mounted infantry. Cavalry proper carried a standard whereas the dragoons carried a guidon.

As well as being the tactical unit, the squadron was also an administrative unit and sometimes treated as a separate entity. The dispositions of the 13th Chasseurs à Cheval is a case in point, in November 1822 its 1st and 4th squadrons were attached to the 'Army of Observation' on the Spanish frontier. On the 30 March, just before the French army entered Spain, it was joined by the 2nd squadron. The 4th squadron was renumbered the 6th squadron and equipped with the lance. Actual returns for the squadrons on the 7 April give a regimental staff of eight officers, 1st squadron, seven officers and 99 NCOs and troopers; 2nd squadron, six officers and 101 NCOs and troopers, 6th squadron, 7 officers and 97 NCOs and troopers. The other three squadrons remained in France. After the campaign, the 13th Chasseurs formed part of the army of occupation in Spain; however the 2nd squadron returned to France and was replaced by the 3rd squadron. They remained in Cadiz until 1828 when they returned by sea to Toulon at a combined strength of 23 officers and 373 NCOs and men and 338 horses. On 1 September of that year the full strength of the regiment now reunited, was 43 officers and 685 NCOs and troopers, but only 463 troop horses.

The heavy cavalry were armed with a long straight bladed sword and a single pistol. Dragoons were armed with a light cavalry sabre, a pair of pistols and a musketoon (see Weapons below). The Chasseurs à Cheval carried the sabre, a pair of pistols and a musketoon. Hussars were similarly armed.

Artillery and Engineers and Veterens

The Royal Artillery had eight regiments of Foot and four of Horse, supported by a regiment of the Train of Artillery. In support of the army were companies of the bridging train' artillery workers; artillery technical troops; the Artillery Train; three regiments of Engineers; 47 companies of veteran troops (*sedentaires*) 11 of which were former NCOs and 36 of fusiliers.

Medical

Lastly the Medical services of staff officers. In the medical service there were four companies of *infirmiers*, ambulance soldiers, each consisting of two officers and 125 men. These companies were raised specially for the Spanish campaign.

Schools

There were two military schools, one built under Napoleon at la Flèche in the Loire valley, and the special training academy of St. Cyr in Brittany, also built on the orders of Napoleon. The final element of the army was the Paris institution of *Les Invalides*, for poor or disabled old soldiers.

Discipline Companies

Soldiers who had committed some offence, not serious enough to be discharged, were sent to the Discipline Companies. There were four companies of fusiliers, who were armed and equipped as for the infantry and four companies of Pioneers, who had committed more serious crimes and were not armed with weapons, only picks and shovels! NCOs, craftsmen and drummers were seconded from the Line regiments and were given the rank one above that they had previously held. Officers, after four years of service were also given a promotion, provided they stayed in the battalion for a further two years.

The official establishment of the French army in October 1822 was 241,000 officers and men.

Flags

The familiar French tricolour standard disappeared with the abdication of Napoleon and the return of the Bourbons. The revolution had initiated a whole range of regimental flag designs with stripes and bars and geometrical patterns, all in various combinations of red, white and blue. The pre-revolutionary army's standards had been plain white for the 'King's colour' and a white cross with an almost infinite variety of colours in the corner squares for the regimental colour. The departmental legions, established in 1815, were presented with standards, one for each of the three battalions, decorated with royal emblems. The reorganisation of 1820 which brought back regiments to the French army had a new design of flag to go with it. It was based on a white silk sheet 80cm square with gold fringes and a border of gold semicircles each enclosing a gold *fleur de lis* emblem, eight on each side. The obverse had, in the centre of the sheet, a gold crown with a red cloth lining over the Bourbon coat of arms of a blue disc with three gold *fleur de lis* surrounded by the collar of the Order of St Louis, itself surrounded by a spray of oak and laurel leaves. Appearing from behind the central design were crossed sceptres of Bourbon royalty in gold. Under the central design, a pale blue scroll. On the reverse a similar spray of oak and laurel leaves in the centre of the sheet, enclosing the words, in gold, LE ROI, AU 3e (the number of the regiment), REGIMENT, D'INFANTERIE. In the corner of the sheet, on both sides, the number of the regiment was displayed in gold. A white cravat, which had been awarded to the departmental legions, was tied to the pole. It had a gold fringe and was secured with a gold cord and tassel. The pole was topped with a gold open spear point enclosing a gold *fleur de lis*. The pole itself was painted white. One standard was issued to each regiment. Each battalion had, in addition, marker flags, (used by the companies to form against when on parade) 40cm square, which was blue for the 1st battalion, red for the 2nd and yellow for the 3rd with, in each case, a large white *fleur de lis* symbol, the same on both sides.

The cavalry regiments were issued with a standard of similar design, a 55cm square white sheet, with the obverse showing a border of gold semicircles with *fleur de lis*, but five instead

Regimental colour of the Swiss Guards regiment number 7 (1st Swiss). (H. Boisselier)

of the infantry's eight. In the centre a blue oval, topped with a gold crown with a red cloth lining, with three *fleur de lis* and surrounded by sprays of oak and laurel leaves in gold. Beneath the central emblem a pale blue scroll. The reverse with an inscription in gold letters, LE ROI, AU REGIMENT, DE CUIRASSIERS (or DRAGONS, CHASSEURS…), DU DAUPHIN (or name). A blue disc edged gold in each of the four corners of the sheet, on both sides. As with the infantry, gold open spear point with a gold *fleur de lis*, white cravat with gold fringes and a white flagpole.

The Guard infantry regiments had a variation of the flags used by the infantry. The Swiss infantry for example had the white sheet with gold decorations, but with the addition of small shields around the central Royal arms displaying the badges of the Swiss cantons. Below the sprays of leaves a pair of clasped hands issuing from clouds and a light blue ribbon with the name of the regiment in gold lettering, e.g. GARDE ROYALE 7e REGIMENT.

Weapons

The arms and equipment carried by the men of the new French army differed little from their Napoleonic forebears, the musket however was an improvement over the 1777 model. It was lightened and had some minor modifications made in 1816 and 1822. This latter model was destined to remain in use until the introduction of the breech loading model of 1866 (commonly called the chassepot, after its designer). Each soldier was allowed 40 cartridges each year for training purposes. The basic model of 1822 was later converted to percussion ignition in place of the flintlock and further transformations included rifling the barrel and replacing the percussion hammer with a breech loading mechanism known as the 'tobacco box' (because of its appearance) which was used by many French second line units in 1870-1871. A number of versions of the basic firearm were in use. The standard infantry musket had a calibre of 17.5mm and fired a ball weighing 19 to the pound used by the mass of the Line in the grenadier and fusilier companies, the voltigeurs and chasseurs carried a slightly lighter version, with the barrel about an inch or two shorter. The infantry cartridge box of black leather contained a wooden block with cut outs for four packets of cartridges, a bottle of oil and had a pocket in the flap to hold spare flints. Straps beneath the box were to store the *bonnet de police*. Cavalry firearms were manufactured in an even lighter version, a carbine with a short barrel which made for easier loading when mounted which was referred to as a musketoon. It had a calibre 17.1mm. Finally most mounted troops carried one or two pistols, with limited range and accuracy, which had almost to touch an enemy to ensure that the ball struck its target.

The artillery used by the French army was based on the Gribeauval system which had been introduced in 1765, simplifying the earlier numbers of barrels, carriages and wheels (over 28 different types). Napoleon had introduced a new system with lighter barrels and simpler carriages in 1803. The Bourbon restoration in 1815 had the political objective of effacing anything connected with the emperor and so the Gribeauval system was reinstated, but still using Napoleonic material. The Inspector-General of Artillery, Count Valée was charged with the reorganisation of the artillery materiel, but his improvements did not appear until 1825.

The light cavalry also received new sabres of the model 1822, which had a three bar hilt and a long curved blade of 92cm. Production did not get under way until July 1823, so few if any would have reached the Spanish theatre. Like the infantry musket, it proved highly popular and some pieces remained in service up to the First World War. The French in Spain carried the light cavalry model Year XI (the revolutionary calendar equivalent to the year 1802-1803) with curved blade and the heavy cavalry model, also Year XI, with straight blade, 95cm long and with a four bar hilt.

3

Spain and the Spanish Armies

Infantry

After the defeat of Napoleon's armies and the re-establishment of the Spanish state under Ferdinand VII, the Spanish army had a line infantry establishment of 48 regiments which included three of Irish origin. A further three regiments were recruited in Switzerland. By 1821 the number of regiments had been reduced to 37. Each regiment had two battalions, each battalion of eight companies including the two elite companies of grenadiers and light infantry known as *cazadores* and six companies of fusiliers. The regiments were given numbers and also kept their titles, which had been re-allocated in the reforms of 1815 (some of the titles had originated in the early 1700s) a number had Royal origins, such as the 'Rey' (the King) and 'Imperial Alexander' (named from the Russian Tsar), others of regional areas, 'Grenada' or 'America'.

The constitutional government which took over the regular army, reorganised the tactical unit to be the battalion rather than the old regimental formations. Each battalion was allocated a number, although the old names were still referred to in reports of battles and army lists.

Each battalion was under the command of a colonel, with the tactical command exercised by the lieutenant colonel. Each battalion consisted one company of grenadiers, one company of *cazadores* and six companies of fusiliers. The two elite companies had five officers, 21 NCOs and 116 men plus three drummers who counted as corporals. The *cazadores* company had three horn signallers in place of the drummers. The fusilier companies had four officers, 20 NCOs and 100 men, plus two drummers. The battalion staff consisted of five officers, a chaplain, a surgeon, a drum major and a master gunsmith.

The Light Infantry battalions had the same organisation, but with the drums replaced by horns.

The regulations laid down that the old names would be retained for the time being, but in case of confusion the number would be used. Each battalion carried a cravat in the Spanish colours on a flagpole beneath a brass lion. In order to save money, which was a commodity in permanently short supply, no battalions were allowed to have a band and senior officers were instructed to keep their uniforms simple without lace

Uniforms, Spanish Regular infantry, drummer, sapper, officer with national colours and *Cazadore* (Light infantry). (Conde de Clonard)

Uniforms, Spanish Regular infantry, sapper, officer with national colours, line infantry grenadier and light company. (Conde de Clonard)

or embroidery. Another innovation introduced by the government was the setting up, in each military district, of a school to teach soldiers to read, write and count. A junior officer, a sergeant, a corporal and two soldiers of each unit would attend the school which was to use the 'Lancaster' method of teaching, that is, those with some schooling to help those of lesser achievements.

The 37 two battalion regiments of regular infantry were now numbered as 'Battalions' 1 to 74. If the old first and second battalions of the Toledo regiment turned up on the same battlefield they could be distinguished by the numbers '37' and '38'. The existing Light Infantry battalions were numbered 1 to 14, with two new battalions, 15 and 16 added to the list.

At the end of the Napoleonic Wars the number of light infantry stood at nearly 50,000 men. This was soon reduced to 12 battalions. In 1818 it was again reduced to just 10 battalions, however in 1821 it was raised to 14. Each battalion had six centre companies, or *cazadores*, with one elite company of *carabineros* (equivalent to the grenadiers of the line infantry) and one company of *tiradores*. The Light infantry were also allocated numbers, but as with the infantry were referred to by their regional names, 'the Light infantry of Aragon', or 'the Light infantry of Valencia'.

The battalions of National Guards were raised on a regional basis and received a number and the name of the town or district where they were formed. For example battalions 1, 2, 3 and 4 had the names 'Jaen', 'Badajoz', 'Sevilla' and 'Burgos' respectively. Depending on the local populations they were either of six or eight companies strong. The total strength of the National Guards was 75 battalions of the Line Infantry and 12 battalions of Light Infantry.

Cavalry

As with the infantry, in 1815 Spanish army had a large number of cavalry regiments, 17 regiments of heavy cavalry which included cuirassiers and lancers. By 1822 just eight regiments of heavy cavalry remained. The cuirassiers were abolished. In 1820 the light cavalry was reorganised by abolishing the hussar regiments and establishing 12 regiments of cavalry called *cazadores*.

Both heavy and light cavalry regiments were composed of four squadrons, each of two companies. In peace time the regiment had 36 officers including a chaplain and surgeon and 555 NCOs and men. The regiment however only included 396 troop horses. Each company was commanded by a captain, supported by a lieutenant and an ensign. Non commissioned ranks included a first sergeant, three second sergeants, a trumpeter, four first corporals and four second corporals and 36 mounted troopers and 19 dismounted troopers. In wartime the strength each company was increased by a further ensign, a second sergeant and 32 mounted troopers. On paper the strength of a regiment stood at 48 officers and 819 NCOs and troopers. Some officers and men were told off to form the cadre of a depot company.

The regimental staff was led by a colonel, a senior lieutenant colonel, two junior lieutenant colonels who acted as squadron commanders (with the administration of two squadrons each), two captains, two second lieutenants, four ensigns (a junior officer rank, not the standard bearer), for NCOs and other ranks there were mounted trumpeters, a saddler, an armourer, and four smiths. On the strength were six horses to pull the regimental forges. One standard was allotted to each regiment. The first company of the first squadron was considered the regimental elite and had an extra NCO. Where the regiment had men serving overseas, on the American continent, they formed a fifth squadron on their return.

In August 1822 a further eight provisional cavalry regiments were formed with a similar organisation to the existing light cavalry regiments. The compliment for each company was 66 officers and troopers giving a regiment a full strength of 528, with 496 horses. Steps were also taken to introduce a breeding program to improve the quality of cavalry horses.

The Constitutional armies were organised on a regional basis. The armies were made up of regular regiments of the Spanish army and numbers of National Militia who were called upon to defend their own districts. In the north Lieutenant-General Ballesteros commanded around 20,000 men facing the main French army coming from Bayonne. At the other end of the Pyrenees, defending Catalonia and Barcelona, Lieutenant-General Mina had a force of 22,000 men. In central Spain, an army of reserve was formed of 18,000 men under Lieutenant-General l'Abisbal. In the north-west Lieutenant-General Morillo had a force of 10,000 men. Another 50,000 men were stationed in garrisons and fortresses across the country. In numbers, an impressive force of 120,000 men, greater than the French army poised to invade. However much of the Constitutional army was employed in dealing with the Royalist counter-insurrections which had broken out all over the country.

Juan Martin Diaz

As well as the regular regiments and the National Militia the Constitutionalists also counted a number of former guerrilla band leaders among their supporters. One of the most famous in the war against Napoleon was Juan Martin Diaz. (*El Empecinado*, the 'Mucky', a nickname applied to inhabitants of his home town, but which could also mean 'the Stubborn', which was more appropriate.) Diaz had raised troops to fight against the French and alongside the English in southern Spain, with little success in the open field, but much more effective in guerrilla actions, so much so that the French organised a special column under General Joseph Hugo to hunt him down. Needless to say they did not succeed. Although he had fought for many years to restore Ferdinand to the throne, he was opposed to the absolute monarchy that Ferdinand tried to impose, even after signing the 1812 Constitution. When Riego raised the banner of revolution, Diaz joined him and was made military governor of Zamora. After 1823, he went into exile in Portugal, but asked for free conduct to return, which was given. However, the Royal authorities went back on their word, arrested him and threw him into prison. He was finally hanged in August 1825. There is a magnificent portrait of Diaz, painted in about 1808 wearing a scarlet hussar uniform, painted by Goya.

Charles Lallamand

The French invasion inspired a number of 'adventurers' to head for Spain to fight for the liberal cause, or to fight against the Bourbons, French and Spanish, not always the same thing. One such adventurer was a Frenchman who had served Napoleon well and had been with him when he was dispatched to St. Helena. Francois-Antoine, or Charles as he preferred, Lallemand, had held the rank of General de Division and was commander of the Chasseurs à Cheval of the Imperial Guard at the battle of Waterloo. Sentenced to death by the Bourbon government, he had escaped to America and had been involved in several French emigré societies before appearing in Spain in 1823 with a mixed bag of fellow adventurers calling themselves the 'Legion of French Refugees'. Little is known of their exploits, but the collapse of the Spanish Constitutionalists ended their career. He escaped to Portugal where he ended up in prison (the Portuguese had had their own failed attempt at a Liberal government). After living in poverty in various parts of Europe, he again sailed for the United States and became a citizen of that country. When Louis Philippe became King of the French, Lallemand was restored to his rank and titles and later became military governor of Corsica.

Jean-Baptiste Carrel and the Foreign Legion

A major problem faced by the French government in 1822, when the *cordon sanitaire* was formed along the Pyrenees and it was clear this would lead to a military intervention in Spain, was just how much could they rely on the loyalty of the army. Many officers, especially at senior level, had been replaced by loyal royalists, that is, men who had left France during the revolutionary and Napoleonic periods, or had at least not served enthusiastically the Imperial regime. Similarly, many NCOs had owed their promotion, which meant their pay, prospects and prestige, to the imperial army and whose loyalty at the very least was suspect. Many imperial officers had been put on half pay, or had their promotion blocked and some NCOs had left the service. Those officers and men remaining were under constant watch by their superiors. Even some younger officers, who joined the service after Waterloo had a marked admiration for the imperial regime, while governed absolutely by Napoleon, had a liberal view on equality before the law and the advancement of the individual by his own talents.

One such man was Jean-Baptiste Carrel. He was born in 1800 and received a good secondary education and entered the military school of St Cyr. He was promoted to sub-lieutenant in the 29th Regiment of Infantry of the Line. In 1823, on the outbreak of the campaign, he resigned from the French army and slipped across the border and made his way to Barcelona. This city was a centre of Spanish constitutional government and acted as a magnet to liberal sympathisers from France, Italy, Poland and other European states (English volunteers generally made their way by sea to Vigo and La Coruna on the Atlantic coast).

In the Biscay provinces, a former ADC to Marshal Ney, Charles Caron, was given the task to organise a battalion of French volunteers under the name of the 'Napoleon II battalion'. This was the company who tried to entice the French on the frontier at the Bidasoa River to desert. In Barcelona, the Spanish General Mina ordered the raising of another company of French volunteers to be formed, also named 'Battalion of Napoleon II', commanded by Captain Maurice Persat, with Carrel made lieutenant, as his second in command. [Napoleon II, the son of the emperor, was then just 12 years old and a cadet in the Austrian army, a virtual prisoner of Metternich, the Austrian chancellor.] The battalion was part of the troops known variously as the Foreign Liberal Legion, or the Foreign Legion, and was composed of French volunteers who were all former soldiers. The French volunteers are reported as wearing the uniform of the old Imperial Guard and carrying a flagpole supporting a large eagle. The French tried to increase their numbers by encouraging deserters from the besiegers of Barcelona, but with little success. The Foreign Legion had two companies of the French volunteers and four or five companies made up of volunteers from the Italian states (Piedmont and Naples principally). A number of supernumerary French NCOs were formed into a company of sharpshooters. The Legion also included a small cavalry element, about 35 men armed with lances.

The Legion took part in the expedition which set out on the night of 9/10 September by fishing boats from Barcelona to attempt to gain the fortress of Figueras and rouse the local population against the invaders. About 2,500 troops under Don Fernandez including the Legion under the Italian Colonel Piechiarotti, fought a running battle with the French for two days until most of them were dispersed and forced to surrender. The French troops of the Napoleon II Battalion were the last to retain their discipline and surrendered as a body of about 100 men, breaking their muskets, but retaining their swords as a defence against the Spanish Royalist 'Soldiers of the Faith' who did not take kindly to prisoners of any description.

The French liberal prisoners were sent back to France under escort and imprisoned in a fortress. Carrel was sentenced to death, but was later to be acquitted and released. He turned to journalism in later years and edited a radical newspaper in Paris. Among his literary efforts was a 'Report on the campaign of Catalonia by a French defector'.

The Army of the Faith

The troops of the Spanish Royalist armies were organised (perhaps not the right word, more properly, disorganised) on a regional basis and tended to stay in their home territory, either to re-establish and maintain royal authority, or assist the French forces in siege operations and co-operating with the French in trying to neutralise the Spanish Constitutional forces. Their numbers varied during the campaign, depending on their success or failure in the field and the reputation of their commanders. Collectively known as 'The Army of the Faith', they never operated as a national force. When Madrid was taken from the Constitutional government, a number of units of infantry and at least one regiment of lancers was raised from among the population. At some time the royalist forces throughout Spain numbered over 30,000 men and were distributed as follows:

Commander	Location	Units
General Quesada	around Madrid	3,500 infantry and 500 cavalry
General Bessieres	between Madrid and Valencia	1,000 infantry and 300 cavalry
General O'Donnell	Basque region	450 men
Count D'Espagne	Navarre and San Sebastian	5,000 infantry
General Fleyres	Aragon, south of the Pyrenees	700 men
General Santos-Ladron	Seville and Cordoba	over 1,000 men
Baron d'Eroles	Catalonia, around Barcelona	8,000 men
General Ramon-Chambo	Valencia, Mediterranean coast	1,000 men
General Elnoy	Tortoas, south of Barcelona	2,000 men
General Sampere	Valencia	1,500 men
General Merino	Estramadura, adjoining Portugal	2,000 men
General Cimeros	La Mancha, south of Madrid	?
General Longa	Santander	6,000 men

There are a large number of 'generals' on the list, not all of them army ranks, but some a courtesy title. Some, however, were experienced officers who had fought the French during the Napoleonic period, for example Baron d'Eroles was a distinguished leader who had gained a number of victories during the war against Napoleon's troops. Baron d'Eroles was a brave and respected officer who attracted a number of volunteers to his forces. Many of the Army of the Faith had no military experience and needed some sort of training to channel their enthusiasm. On the 1 April about one thousand men had been gathered at a camp at Saint-Esteve, near Perpignan in southern France, just over the border from Spain. On the 5 April they were given arms by the French. Among the volunteers, those who had been made officers or NCOs, were a few who had military experience and were given the task to instruct the mass of volunteers. To teach them the men were formed into a square of about 100, with one side open where the instructor took his place. He then went through the drill of loading and firing while the men followed his movements. The volunteers were also given uniforms by the French authorities, although no regulations have been found, it is probable that they were given uniforms resembling the French light infantry, as other units were later in the campaign. The men taught themselves drill, in small groups of five or six, learning the cadence of step. They were never able to manoeuvre as a battalion and hardly ever even as companies. After just three weeks the volunteers left the camp to accompany the French forces in the campaign in Catalonia, for them the real training now commenced.

The French government took the training of these volunteers seriously, the minister of war, the Duke of Belluno (Marshall Victor-Perrin), sent Colonel Maurice de Roquemaurel to Baron d'Eroles to supervise their training and organisation. This

Spanish volunteers.
(As depicted by Professor
Richard Knotel)

officer had led a chequered military career, after military school, he was appointed a second lieutenant in the Dauphiné infantry regiment, but emigrated in 1791 to join the French royalist army, under the Prince de Condé in Austria. When it disbanded he moved to England and made his living giving fencing lessons. In 1798 he was in Austria again. However in 1800 he returned to France and enlisted in a regiment of hussars, rising from private to corporal to second lieutenant (again) in 1802. This part of his military life was brief, the following year his father demanded that he return to look after the family property (which included getting married and starting a family) which was in the foothills of the Pyrenees a little to the north-west of Andorra. When the French invaded Spain in 1808, bands of Spanish guerrillas crossed the border from Catalonia and raided French farms and villages. De Roquemaurel was appointed to command the local defence forces, taking the fight across the frontier to the Spanish, and learning to use guerrilla tactics with outstanding success. In 1812, for his exploits, he was awarded the Knights Cross of the Legion of Honour. Although he welcomed the return of the Bourbons in 1815 he was distrusted due to the service he given the Imperial regime and was retired on half pay with the rank of colonel. His undoubted military talents led to his recall in 1823 and being seconded

Soldiers of the Royalist
'Army of the Faith'.
(Open source)

to the Baron d'Eroles. During an engagement with Spanish troops he was shot in the chest, but his life was saved by a leather wallet in his breast pocket and the cross of the Legion of Honour pinned to the front of his uniform! Two of his sons, Edouard and Gustave, both joined the Spanish royalist forces and both became officers in the Spanish royal guard.

What became of the French government's generosity to the Spanish royalists was observed by an officer of the French Chasseurs à Cheval later in the year when the campaign was all but over. What he found was not to his liking at all:

> I was curious to visit the camp of St. Roch, near Algeciras, on the road from Cadiz to Gibraltar: I wanted to see Spanish warriors, I saw only beggars; Farther on they were no more than Englishmen, whose handsome demeanour and noble and urban manners contrasted cruelly in the midst of an army almost savage, displaying its miseries with a sort of pride. It had not been more than two months since several Spanish regiments had been organised in the French style, among others that of the Queen; All had been furnished according to the models of our light infantry, everything was new and of the best qualities; Well,

when I saw them, I had no other model to crush the uniform of this body than the enclosed soldier [see illustration below left]. It was the best kept of the whole band. Many had sold their arms, or left them in a state incapable of firing; The officers themselves took leave without leave and appeared in magazines with costumes of fantasy, often ridiculous...

He also observed a troop of lancers who had escorted Ferdinand on his return to Madrid, '....a superb corps which, perfectly equipped for the return of the king to the capital, six months later was in rags and without boots.'

The Royalist units raised in opposition to the Constitutional government were given names which reflected their loyalty, or a regional title. The list is headed by the 'Loyal Guides of the King'; 'The Defenders of the King'; 'Provisional Regiment of the King' and 'The Light Infantry of the King'. The queen and the princes were also used as titles. Regional titles also appeared 'The Loyalists of Sagunto'; 'The Loyalists of Cordoba'; '1st Volunteers of Navarra'. In total 55 units were raised, of various sizes and effectiveness.

With the failure of the revolution after the French invasion of 1823 the whole Spanish army was reorganised. All the regiments which had joined the revolutionary

A Spanish officer dressed in a French Light infantry uniform. (Clerjon de Champagny)

Spanish Royalist cavalry officer. (Clerjon de Champagny)

forces were disbanded and new regiments raised in their place. In 1824 the new army consisted of eight regiments of Line infantry, later increased to 10, and five battalions of Light Infantry, later raised to six. Their personnel was drawn from the royalist regiments who had fought against the Constitutionalists.

The pre-revolutionary Spanish army had a number of regiments drawn from personnel from foreign countries, Naples, Ireland and Switzerland and on 20 March 1824 three regiments were raised from Swiss nationals, the Regiments Wimpffen, Kayser and Zey. They remained a separate organisation and not part of the national establishment.

Flags

Spanish lancer specially equipped to escort
Ferdinand on his return to Madrid.
(Clerjon de Champagny)

The Spanish army tried to organise a militia in 1814, but due to lack of finances the militia was not formally brought into being until 1820 after the start of the revolution. At that time some of the militia battalions were presented with purple flags, but these were later replaced by the Spanish national colours of red, yellow and red. The colours were arranged in three equal horizontal bands with yellow in the middle. The name of the battalion was written on the top red band of the flags with the word *CONSTITUCION* in the central yellow portion. The reverse of the flag carried a Spanish coat of arms with a crown and a bull's head motif in each of the four corners.

During the Napoleonic Wars the Spanish army carried flags of an old pattern decorated with a St Andrews ragged cross, the cross of Burgundy, with various Royal emblems. The revolution of 1820 swept away the Royal symbols and also the flag itself. Each regiment was led by an officer carrying a flagpole topped with the symbol of Spain a, bronze lion, and tied beneath the lion a long cravat in the national Spanish colours of red, yellow, red. After the crushing of the revolution new standards were issued, in the style of the old flags. It was not until 1843 that the red/yellow/red flags were introduced, the name of the regiment being shown on the new standard. When the Duke of Angoulême entered the Spanish capital to install the royal government (albeit without the king for the time being), as a gesture of goodwill the French brought with them from Paris about 50 regimental standards captured during the

1808 invasion and, with due ceremony, handed them back to the Spanish at a special parade in Madrid. They were not issued or used by the Spanish Royalist regiments or the newly rebuilt army after 1823.

Ranks

Badges of rank for officers in the Spanish Constitutional army, authorised in January 1823, were a single epaulette on the left shoulder with a contra epaulette on the right shoulder for a sub-lieutenant and for a lieutenant a fringed epaulette on the right shoulder with a contra epaulette on the left. The captain had a fringed epaulette on each shoulder. The fringes were of fine silk material and the straps of flat braid. For field offices a similar system with a fringed epaulette on the left shoulder for a major, fringed epaulette on the right shoulder for a Lieutenant-Colonel with a contra epaulette on the opposite shoulder and two fringed epaulettes for a colonel. The fringes for field officers were of all the bullion type and the braided straps were of twisted material.

For senior Sergeants epaulettes with gold fringes on each shoulder, for junior Sergeants a similar epaulette on the right shoulder with a contra epaulette on the left. A corporal wore three stripes of yellow braid on the cuff, a lance corporal (equivalent) two yellow stripes and a senior private one yellow stripe.

4

The campaign of the French Army to Madrid and beyond

The Congress of Verona

There were two diseases affecting Spain which caused great concern to the French government. The first was the yellow fever and the second was revolutionary fervour. To prevent either, or both, crossing the border, a *cordon sanitaire* was established along the Pyrenees frontier. As the political situation in Spain worsened, the cordon was strengthened and became an Army of Observation.

The Congress of Verona, sitting in October 1822, consisting of the Quadruple Alliance (one of the European alliances set up after the battle of Waterloo to maintain the peace) made up of Britain, France, Austria and the Netherlands gave France permission to intervene in Spain and restore Ferdinand to his dignity of absolute ruler. The Holy Alliance of Russia, Austria and Prussia had earlier refused Ferdinand's appeal for help (presumably because of the difficulty of getting troops to Spain without crossing the territory of another state, even though the Russians offered to send an army to protect France while her army was restoring the former situation in Spain.)

The Congress had demanded that the Spanish king be restored to his full powers but as it was rebuffed by the Cortes, the army in the Pyrenees based largely around the city of Bayonne and the west coastal region now became an Army of Invasion. The European ministers' terms became even more demanding and the British government advised the Spaniards to accept the terms and offered to mediate. The Cortes however remained intransigent and diplomatic relations were severed. The French army now prepared to cross the frontier and restore the king by force of arms. The French commander, the Duke of Angoulême, son of the future King

Louis Antoine d'Artois Duke of Angoulême. (Contemporary painting by an unknown artist)

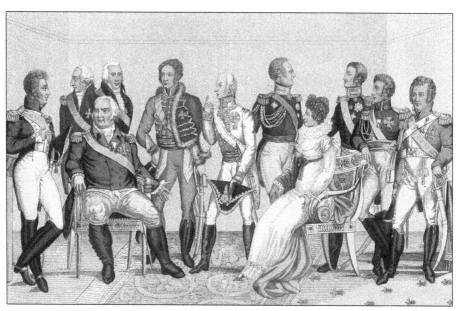

French Royal family and Sovereigns of Europe, contemporary print, King Louis XVIII seated on the left and the Duke of Angoulême standing, second from the right. (Open source)

Cartoon, '...pushed into war'. (Cruikshank)

Cartoon, 'It's war'. (Cruikshank)

Cartoon, Napoleon's son ready to catch the crown? (Cruikshank)

Charles X, issued a proclamation to the Spanish population, stating the intention of the French army was to restore the king to his throne and deliver Spain from the 'evils of revolution'.

Composition of the French Army

The French Army of the Pyrenees, formed to invade Spain, consisted of five corps with the addition of a Reserve. Under the Duke of Angoulême, the Chief of Staff was Lieutenant-General the Count Guilleminot, the chief of artillery Lieutenant-General Viscount Tirlet and the chief engineer, Lieutenant-General Viscount de la Brunerie. Each corps was organised into divisions divided into brigades of Line and Light infantry with light cavalry detachments.

The First Corps under Marshal Oudinot, Duke of Reggio, contained three infantry divisions and a division of dragoons. Chief of Staff Count Grundler.

Division	Commander	Brigade	Infantry Regiment	Cavalry Regiment
1st	D'Autichamp	Vallin	9th Light	13th and 14th Chasseurs
		Saint-Hilaire	23rd and 28th Line	
		Berthier	37th and 38th Line	
2nd	Bourck	De La Rochejacquelein	7th Light	7th Chasseurs and 1st Hussars
		D'Albignac	15th and 22nd Line	
		De Marguerye	30th and 35th Line	
4th	Obert	Vitre	2nd Light	9th Chasseurs and 5th Hussars
		Toussaint	20th and 27th Line	
		Goujeon	34th and 36th Line	
1st Dragoons	Castex	Prince de Carignan		2nd and 8th Dragoons
		Saint-Priest		7th and 9th Dragoons
			42 battalions	40 squadrons

Charles Albert, the Prince of Carignan, heir to the throne of Piedmont-Sardinia, had become involved in a 'liberal' uprising at Turin in 1821 and the king, Charles Felix, suspected that he might harbour further liberal intentions against the absolute monarchy had considered excluding him from the succession. Charles Albert took the opportunity of the French invasion to demonstrate his absolutist credentials by joining the French army and was given command of a brigade of cavalry; he also acted as a staff officer for the Chief of Staff of the Army.

The Second Corps was commanded by Count Molitor and consisted of two infantry divisions and a dragoon division. Chief of Staff, De Borelli.

French Aides de Camp, after Lucien Rousselot. (Open source)

French infantry musicians. (Henri Boisselier)

French Infantry officer. (Hippolyte Bellangé)

French grenadier officer. (Eugene Lami)

Division	Commander	Brigade	Infantry Regiment	Cavalry Regiment
3rd	Loverdo	Bonnemains Corsin Ordonneau	4th Light 1st and 11th Line 12th and 29th Line	10th and 19th Chasseurs
6th	Pamphile- Lacroix	Saint-Chamans D'Arbaud-Joucques Pelleport	8th Light 4th and 13th Line 24th and 39th Line	4th and 20th Chasseurs
2nd Dragoons	Domon	Vincent Faverot		3rd and 5th Dragoons 4th and 10th Dragoons
			28 battalions	32 squadrons

The Prince of Hohenlohe commanded the Third Corps with Count Meynadier as his chief of staff. The corps had two infantry divisions.

Division	Commander	Brigade	Infantry Regiment	Cavalry Regiment
7th	De Conchy	Potier Janin Quinsonas	3rd Light and 6th Line 9th and 14th Line	2nd Hussars and 12th Chasseurs
8th	Canuel	Huber Schoeffer Bruny	5th Light and 17th Line 21st and 25th Line	4th and 20th Chasseurs
			22 battalions	16 squadrons

Added to this corps was a division of Spanish Royalists.

The Fourth Corps was led by Marshal Moncey, the Duke de Conegliano, with Desprez as chief of staff. The corps had three infantry divisions.

Division	Commander	Brigade	Infantry Regiment	Cavalry Regiment
5th	Curial	De Vence Picot de Peccadeuc Vasserot	6th Light 7th and 18th Line 26th and 32nd Line	18th and 23rd Chasseurs
9th	Damas	De Montgarde De Maringoue Rastignac	5th Light and 17th Line 8th and 31st Line	6th and 22nd Chasseurs
10th	Donnadieu	Des Odoarts Saint-Priest La Tour-Du-Pin	1st Light and 2nd Line 3rd and 19th Line	5th Chasseurs and 6th Hussars
			36 battalions	24 squadrons

The Fifth Corps, commanded by Marshal Lauriston with Saint-Cyr-Nuges as chief of staff. Only two divisions made up this corps.

Division	Commander	Brigade	Infantry Regiment	Cavalry Regiment
11th	Ricard	De Chastellux		3rd Chasseurs and 3rd Hussars
		Rapatel	19th Light and 41st Line	
		Tromelin	16th and 60th Line	
12th	Pecheux	Danremont	2nd Light and 33rd Line	
		Fernig	10th and 40th Line	
			22 battalions	8 squadrons

There are other versions of the French Order of Battle, most agree with the one above, but they are obviously copies, or all taken from an 'official' document, another source gives a slightly different version in the distribution of regiments within the brigades, but it is incomplete.

The Reserve Corps was made up of contingents from the Royal Guard and a division of heavy cavalry. Its commander was Count Bordesoulle with the Count of Bourbon-Busset as chief of staff. The first contingent consisted of three squadrons of the Garde-du-Corps of the King and of Monsieur. The infantry contingent was formed from drafts from the 3rd, 6th and 7th (1st Swiss) Regiments of the Royal Guard comprising a total strength of eight battalions (similar to the *regiments de marche* created during Franco-Prussian war) commanded by the Count de Bourmont. The cavalry brigade had four squadrons each from the 2nd Guard Cuirassiers, the Guard Chasseurs and the Guard Dragoons. They were commanded by Foissac-Latour. The heavy cavalry division consisted of eight squadrons taken from the 2nd, 4th, 5th and 6th Cuirassiers under Viscount Roussel. The artillery of the Guard, commanded by Colonel De Laporte consisted of the 1st Company of Foot Artillery and the 1st Company of Horse Artillery.

The headquarters was escorted by detachments from the gendarmerie from the Elite Gendarmes, from the Gendarmes of Paris and from the Departmental Legions. There was also a small detachment from the Foreign Regiment of Hohenlohe. The troops stationed along the frontier and ready to march consisted of the following numbers; First Corps 27,485 men 5,879 horses and 24 guns. The Second Corps had 20,312 men 4,984 horses and 12 guns. The Third Corps 16,076 men, 2,700 horses and 12 artillery pieces, attached to this corps was a division of Spanish royalists under the command of the Count D'Espagne, which then amounted about 5,000 men. The Fourth Corps stood at 21,099 men, 4,376 horses and 24 guns. Finally the Reserve Corps at 9,690 men 3,470 horses and 24 guns.

The V Corps, shown in the table, started life as the Second Reserve Corps, but, later in the campaign, was given a more official designation.

These formations were not fixed; columns could be made up ad hoc for a specific task, to shadow a Constitutional army, or to blockade a fortress, for example.

Descriptions of battles and sieges, as far as the French accounts are concerned, sometimes refer to the division or its commander, but for many actions the unit is described by the name of the brigade commander. These officers, the lowest level of general, could also be given semi-independent roles with battalions drawn from

French voltigeur. (Eugene Lami)

Swiss Guards, 8th Regiment. (Henri Boisselier)

different divisions, or even corps. Also, as the war progressed, there were changes of personnel, retirements and promotions. As the war drew to a close, new formations were organised which would act as an Army of Occupation, an occupation that in some cases lasted five years.

The total for the assembled army was 76,381 infantry, 21,409 cavalry and 96 pieces of artillery. The number of men comes to almost 98,000, but these figures were obtained by counting the numbers of battalions, squadrons and batteries listed in the orders of battle for each corps and multiplying by the official complement, other sources give quite different and much lower figures [See Bibliography, *Victoires Conquetes Desastres, Revers et Guerres Civiles des Francais*] the First Corps for example actually mustered just over 21,000 infantry and 3,700 cavalry and Hohenlohe's Third Corps counted a little under 9,000 infantry and 1,500 cavalry. In one case where a regimental history does give precise numbers, that of the 4th Light, it consisted of two battalions totalling 47 officers and 1,148 NCOs and men.

Not quite the 100,000 men boasted of by the French king, probably nearer 80,000 men. But hopefully sufficient for the task they had been set. The Duke of Angoulême was no mere Royal figurehead, but a principled and conscientious man, with some military experience, who carried out his instructions with energy. He, and his staff, were aware of the problems that had faced by Napoleon's invading army and determined to keep their troops well supplied from home and if they could not the troops were paid promptly so that they could buy what they needed from the local populace. This had a splendid effect on the areas where the French army passed through. They also had the tremendous advantage that they generally had the support of the local people, who had a great reverence for King Ferdinand and no sympathy for the

Cartoon, the Duke of Angouleme caught with his trousers down.
(Unknown artist, published in London, April 1823)

'liberal' constitutionalists. Bands of guerrillas were formed, but acting as allies of the French. The main French army prepared to advance from Bayonne towards San Sebastian, while the corps of Marshal Moncey was stationed at the east end of the Pyrenees, on the Mediterranean coast with the object of taking Barcelona, which was held by a strong garrison of Spanish constitutionalists.

A French sergeant gives a description of the civil war then raging across the frontier, where the regular troops loyal to the Cortes attempted to disperse various Royalist bands that were infesting the province.

> Our object was no longer to preserve France from the contagion that afflicted Barcelona, but to prevent the civil war that was going on in Catalonia and Navarre from spreading disorder to our side of the frontiers. Precautions increased the more that the Constitutionalists defeated the Absolutists; and, in fact, the latter would in all probability have been completely annihilated had they not been able to find an inviolable shelter in the French territory. They came to us in bands, all covered with filth and rags, and then soon took flight again for Spain, whence they were driven back by new defeats behind our lines.[1]

---

1   Robert Guillemard, *Adventures of a French Sergeant, during his campaigns in Italy, Spain, Germany etc. from 1803 to 1823* (London: Henry Colburn, 1826).

These were the official formations of the French army poised to advance into Spanish territory however, as the campaign progressed, divisions and brigades where given specific tasks, ad hoc forces were organised under whatever generals were available to attack enemy strong points; guard strategic positions or undertake sieges against towns and fortresses held by the Spanish constitutional armies. During the advance it was proved to be necessary to reduce several fortresses for which a siege train and artillery park and numbers of engineer companies were employed.

The build-up of troops, stores and horses and particularly transport wagons continued from the beginning of 1823, the organisation now in the capable hands of the financier Ouvrard. By the beginning of April the orders to advance had been prepared. Events came to a head on 6 April, when a group (not an organised unit) of about 100 French and Piedmontese liberal supporters, dressed in the uniforms of Napoleon's Old Guard and carrying a large French tricolour flag appeared on the south bank of the Bidasoa River and tried to goad the French troops opposite them to desert. The 9th Light of the 1st Division of Oudinot's First Corps, were somewhat nonplussed by their antics until the brigade commander, General Louis Vallin, arrived to see what was going on. He ordered the troops to open musket fire and a battery of artillery to load with grapeshot. The discharge laid a number of the Liberals low and the rest decided to disperse. They later joined with other non-Spanish Liberal supporters under Sir Robert Wilson (an experienced British officer who had fought under Wellington), or the Belgian Janssens, to form a Liberal Legion. An eyewitness to the crossing on that morning says that after the discharge of grapeshot:

> Some companies of light infantry threw themselves into boats, and [crossed over into] Spain. The wounded were brought back to the shore of France. They survived only a few hours with their wounds. I was particularly struck by the appearance of one of the victims of this memorable morning. He was a man of 36, a noble and proud figure. During three hours of his agony, all the questions addressed to him were in vain; he answered them only by prayers in Latin, in order, no doubt, to be ignorant of the nation he belonged to. From that moment I hate[d] politics [which seemed to be] always in opposition to the principles of humanity. In the pockets of this unfortunate man were found proclamations and the epaulettes of a superior officer. I shall never forget this man. He was still a fanatic.[2]

First Blood

The following day the French army began its invasion of Spain, the first troops wading across the river, the cavalry finding a ford and the artillery using a quickly assembled pontoon bridge. The original stone bridge had been destroyed during the

2   Jules Clerjon de Champagny, *Album d'un soldat pendant la campagne d'Espagne en 1823*, Paris, 1829.

Napoleonic war and had not yet been rebuilt. The Spanish Constitutionalist troops to the south of the river, a battalion of the Imperial Alexander Regiment, retreated before them. As with soldiers of any army and any country at any time, the French were keen to communicate with the locals for a number of reasons. Unfortunately the locals in this part of Spain were not Spanish speaking but were native Basques. Our eyewitness was not impressed, even though some men managed a phrase or two. He says, of the local inhabitants:

> Their savage language is more unintelligible than Low-Breton; I have never heard a single word that has anything to do with the equivalent of any known language. *Inda sou mou souba* (you want to kiss me), is the sentence most easily remembered by our chasseurs and hussars, and certainly they could repeat it on all the rest of the globe without fear of making the young blush red.

As the political aim of the invasion was to restore Ferdinand to his throne, the French plan was simply to march to Madrid, release Ferdinand from his captivity, re-establish his government and then go home. Even before the start of the campaign, some members of the French administration were saying that the whole idea was just too costly for the not-so-full treasury to sustain. However, politically, the decision had been made, so whatever the cost the war had to be carried to its conclusion.

The Constitutionalists raised armies for the defence of the country, not as a national force, but to cover the various districts (or historical kingdoms) into which Spain was divided. General Francisco Espoz y Mina, a successful guerrilla leader during Napoleon's occupation of Spain, was given command in Catalonia. The capital and seat of the king and government at Madrid was placed under the protection of Enrique O'Donnell, Count of Abisbal, who although an aristocrat was against the French invasion. General Francisco Ballesteros another successful officer during the campaign against the Imperial French was to cover the eastern provinces of Aragon, Valencia and Murcia. The northern provinces of Galicia and Asturias were entrusted to Pablo Morillo y Morillo, Count of Cartagena and Marquess of La Puerta. Pedro Villacampa y Maza de Lizana was charged with the formation of an army of reserve in Andalusia, far from the French advance. The only plan seemed to be to avoid battle, but for Ballesteros and Morillo to harass the French with frequent skirmishes to weaken them enough so that they would halt their advance.

7 April 1823

After the dispersal of the French and Italian liberals, the First Corps, led by Vallin's brigade, crossed over the river to the Spanish side. The Second Corps of Molitor followed, while the Third Corps of Prince Hohenlohe crossed further upstream. The Spanish detachments which had been posted along the frontier retired to the fortress of San Sebastian. The fortress was commanded by Don Pablo de la Pena with about 3,000 men. As well as the battalion of the Imperial Alexander Regiment (Number 45 in the Spanish service), there was also a battalion of the Valencey Regiment (Number 42) and companies from the Espana (Number 18) and Salamanca Regiments and a force of 1,200 militia. As the army set out on its march to the next objective, Vitoria, the division of General Bourck (a decedent of an Irish family who had fled to France with James II in 1688 after the battle of the Boyne) was detached to take San Sebastian. Bourck sent a parliamentary to demand the surrender of the fortress which was rebuffed. The French infantry attempted to storm the fortress, unsuccessfully, with the Spanish mounting a counter-attack. This was in turn thrown back by detachments of the 22nd, 35th and 36th Line Infantry. As this was the first serious action of the campaign, the Duke of Angoulême personally congratulated those who were deemed to have behaved bravely under fire. When reviewing the soldiers in front of San Sebastian, a stray bullet landed close by and threw up dust over his uniform. His calm reaction did much to improve his reputation among the troops. Rather than sit down in front of the fortress and delay the advance, a blockade was declared, albeit rather loosely applied, with a number of regiments under the command of the Prince of Hohenlohe.

True to his published intentions the Duke of Angoulême set up a Spanish administration to govern those provinces which French arms had 'liberated' from the rule of the Cortes. Its first act was to issue a proclamation, which concluded with the declaration that any Spanish government acts passed by the Cortes promulgated after 7 March 1820 would be null and void.

The Advance continues

The French army marched from San Sebastian to the town of Tolosa, where the Second Corps under General Molitor was detached from the main force and headed south-east towards Saragossa, to establish communications between the Duke of Angoulême and the Fourth Corps of General Moncey which was to operate in Catalonia with the object of securing Barcelona from the Constitutional army. The Duke set his forces toward Vitoria, with Madrid as his goal. Thus far no Spanish Constitutionalist troops challenged his march, indeed the only Spanish under arms in the area was a Spanish Royalist division under Lieutenant-General Count d'Espagne numbering around 8,000 men. The French established their headquarters in the town of Vitoria, while the blockade was set up against the Spanish garrison at San Sebastian. The Duke was loath to continue with enemy troops in his rear who might at any time strike at his lines of communications.

The French advanced almost timidly, despite their great strength, as they had no real knowledge of the intentions of the Spanish, who either retreated precipitously before them, or fought desperately to defend some position or other. An easily defended position covering a main bridge over the river Ebro (a major obstacle on the route to Madrid) was left open, if contested would have led a major delay on the French advance, while a small Spanish force at the town of Logrono (also on the Ebro) had to be ejected by house to house fighting. The most likely explanation is that the Spanish had no overall plan and it was left to the field commanders to use their initiative to decide what action to take. There is little evidence of much cooperation among the Constitutional generals and more evidence of distrust and rivalry which made coherent strategy next to impossible.

Logrono

On the 18th April, the French 4th Division of General Obert (part of Marshal Oudinot, the Duke of Reggio's I Corps) advanced upon Logrono to find 1,000 Spaniards, including 200 cavalry under General Don Julian Sanchez, arrayed before the town and obviously intending to dispute the French occupation of the position. As at San Sebastian, the French sent a flag of truce to the Spanish lines summoning them to surrender, which was rebuffed. The French attack was led by the voltigeur company of the 20th Line infantry followed by the division's I Brigade consisting of the 2nd Light Infantry and a regiment of Chasseurs à Cheval and a regiment of hussars, which was stubbornly resisted by the Spanish, who, badly outnumbered, were slowly pushed back into the town. The French were faced with a narrow bridge leading to the town gate which was swept by the fire of the defenders. The French took the barricades of the gate, but found a further gate beyond it.

At this point a teenaged drummer of the 20th of the Line clambered, or was assisted, over the inner wall, and opened the gate from the inside. Colonel de Muller of the 5th Hussars charged through the entrance with two squadrons and a squadron of the lance armed Chasseurs and swept through the main streets, tumbling the Spanish infantry to right and left. There followed a bitter house to house combat as the French infantry following the mounted troops had to clear the town at close quarters. Almost at the gate leading out of the opposite side of the town detachments of the Spanish infantry attempted to form square against the cavalry, but Colonel de Muller charged them and broke their formation, with the infantrymen flying in all directions. De Muller fell badly wounded by two bayonet thrusts and later died of his wounds, but by his actions had won the victory. The Spanish again attempted to reform behind the town, assisted by a reinforcement of a further 200 horsemen from the Bourbon and The Queen cavalry regiments, but the French Chasseurs and Hussars continued their victorious action and they fled before them.

The Spanish lost two hundred men as prisoners, including the general, Don Julian Sanchez, and a quantity of small arms and about 30 bodies were found after the battle. The French admitted to only two officers and two horsemen wounded, but this surely hid a much greater loss. On the 22nd the Duke of Angoulême ordered that those who had contributed to the success at Logrono should receive recognition, de Muller, who was already an officer of the Legion of Honour was promoted to a Commander of the order and Drummer Matreau of the 20th Line for his exploits received the Legion of Honour.

Original sketch for the 'opening of the gate of Logrono'. (Open source)

Operations of Hohenlohe's Corps

As the Duke of Angoulême proceeded towards Madrid, the III Corps under the command of Prince Louis of Hohenlohe, was left to guard the lines of communication with France and to cover the Spanish fortresses which held out in favour of the Cortes. The Prince established his headquarters at Vitoria so he could watch the Spanish garrisons of St. Sebastian and Santona, on the Biscay coast and Pamplona (Pampeluna) the capital of the county of Navarre, halfway between the frontier on the Pyrenees and the river Ebro. Santona was a small city on the northern coast of Spain, but a major base of the Spanish navy. It had a large port with a deep anchorage and was well fortified with a large garrison. A small French squadron cruised outside the entrance to the harbour consisting of a corvette, a gun-brig, two cutters and five galleys, two of which were manned by Spanish royalists. Ships still tried to evade the blockade and as late as 21 September, an English ship, the Eliza, was prevented from entering the port.

The Constitutionalist troops were not content to remain behind their defences, but, on 2 July, made a sortie against the French lines. Supported by artillery fire from the fortress, a battalion strong force, was sent by boat to a beach opposite the fortress and formed into three columns to attack the French outposts, forcing them to give way. A fire fight developed between the Spanish and three companies from the French 21st and 35th of the Line. It was the intervention of another company of the 21st, taking the Spanish in flank, which decide the issue. The Spanish returned to their boats and re-embarked, still covered by artillery fire. Casualty figures are not known, the French admitted to two men killed and eight wounded, while inflicting 50 casualties on the Spanish. The French were also not content to merely blockade the town; one of the Spanish posts in front of the batteries was attacked on the night of 22/23 August by 40 men from the elite companies of the 5th Light Infantry, carabineers and voltigeurs. After successfully capturing the post and chasing off the defenders, they retired to their own lines bringing with them five prisoners. Santona held out against the blockade until the 28th September, when it finally surrendered to the French.

The Duke of Angoulême lingered at Vitoria for some time until on the 10 May, sure of his flanks, he moved on to Burgos. General Molitor marched to Zaragoza (Saragossa) which took the attention of Ballesteros and Morillo gave way before the mass of the French army. He now deemed the way clear and the French army, by steady marches took the road to Madrid. Arriving before the capital on the 20 May, but were preceded by a force of the Spanish 'Army of the Faith' who attempted to capture the city before the French could gain entry. The commander of the Constitutional soldiers in Madrid, General José Pascual de Zayas y Chacón, had about 5,000 men he could rely on and resolved that a convention be concluded so that he could withdraw them without conflict. Jorge Bessières, who had been advancing with a Royalist column alongside the French, lead about one thousand men and tried to storm one the city gates, much to the anger of Zayas who was waiting for the French and feared a bloody reaction from the Royalists against the supporters of the Cortes within Madrid. Zayas tried to reason with Bessières, though without success and his only option was to fight. He attacked the Royalists and made only a little progress until he brought up his artillery which disordered the ranks of the Royalists, who then succumbed to a cavalry charge. The whole of the Royalist column were killed, wounded or taken prisoner. As a result the leading French units, part of the 4th Division of General Obert, was urged to hurry its march and entered Madrid on the morning of the 23 May.

As soon as the Duke of Angoulême entered Madrid, he asked the Spanish Royalists to form a regency government until such time as Ferdinand was able to conduct the affairs of state. This constituted the government of Spain until the king was released from his confinement in Cadiz on 1 October.

According to the convention agreed by General Zayas, the garrison of Madrid was free to march without hindrance until the afternoon of the 26 May. Major-General Vallin with the advance guard of the First Corps was ordered to pursue the Spanish and try to overtake them. He set off by forced marches with the 9th Light and two regiments of cavalry, the 5th Hussars and the 9th Chasseurs and a section of horse artillery. Two days and a night later they caught up with Zayas' rearguard at Talavera on the River Tagus, where they had taken up a defensive position. The French took the initiative and attacked the Spanish, eventually turning the position by the infantry crossing the river by forcing a bridge and the hussars by a ford. Most

Uniforms of the Madrid Royalist volunteers. (Unknown artist)

of the Constitutionalists managed to get away, but lost some prisoners and part of their baggage.

Now in firm control of Madrid, the Duke of Angoulême felt emboldened to divide his army into smaller units and spread them across the country. A column under Lieutenant General Bourdesoulle, made up of the 1st Reserve Division and consisting of troops from the Royal Guard was ordered to make a sweep of the country towards Cordoba and Seville and destroy any troops still loyal to the Cortez. A second column under Lieutenant General Bourmont, supported by a Spanish Royalist brigade, marched into the border region between Spain and Portugal. These two columns were acting apart from the main French army and were given the title of the 'Army of Andalusia'.

The column under General Bourdesoulle, crossing another chain of mountains, on the 7th June faced a militia band under a former guerrilla leader who had fought the French in 1808 to 1814, Colonel Francisco Abad Moreno, nicknamed El Chaleco. The Spanish fell back before him on their main body under General Placentia. The French used their cavalry to good effect and the Spanish retreated. Two days later the French advance guard under the Duke de Dino again attacked the Spanish, who this time fought from a strong position. Among the Spanish was a battalion of regulars from the 'America' Regiment. The French, led by the 2nd Light and supported by the Chasseurs à Cheval of the Royal Guard, advanced into a very heavy fire and later admitted to several killed, including two or three officers and over 40 men wounded. The French arrived at Cordoba on the 13th to find it had been abandoned by the Constitutionalists and the Royalists had taken control.

General Bourmont's column advanced slowly and a Spanish band under the guerrilla leader, the 'Empecinado' attempted to harass his flank, but was kept at bay by the Spanish Royalist auxiliaries. The city of Seville reacted to the departure of the Constitutionalists in a manner similar to Cordoba, and proclaimed its adherence to the Royalist cause, however a brigade under a leader loyal to the Cortes, General Lopez-Banos, entered the city and obliged the citizens, under the barrels of his artillery to resupply his men with money, clothing and equipment. Although pursued by the French, Lopez-Banos managed to reach the coast and leaving his light infantry and cavalry to make for the mountains to form a guerrilla band, took the bulk of his command, about 2,500 men, by boat to Cadiz. The two French columns marched together and on 24 June the Army of Andalusia arrived before Cadiz, where the last acts of the war were to take place.

On the 1st July a ceremony took place in Madrid, in the palace of the king. The King of France, wishing to show to the Spanish people his good will ordered that Spanish regimental standards captured during Napoleon's campaign, and held in Paris, were to be returned. The French had actually taken 92 flags during the period 1808 to 1812, but in 1815 as the Prussians entered Paris 44 of them had been hidden.[3] The remaining 48 were taken from the French archives and together with two taken from the Constitutional forces in early 1823, were handed back to the Royalist Regency. They were not passed on to the new Spanish Royalist regiments, but put up in the Ministry of War in Madrid.

The Duke of Angoulême, on 24th July, made an executive order which designated the military leadership of the Spanish provinces:

1. Leon and Castile and the north-western provinces, Marshal Oudinot, Duke of Reggio, (commander of the I French Army Corps), headquarters in Madrid.
2. Santander, Biscay including those fortresses still in Spanish hands, the Prince of Hohenlohe (commander of the III army Corps), headquarters in Vitoria.
3. Navarra and Aragon, those provinces lying to the south of the Pyrenees, Marshal Lauriston (commander of the II Reserve Corps), headquarters at Tolosa.
4. Valencia, Murcia and Granada, those provinces on the Mediterranean coast, Count Molitor, (commander of the II Corps),
5. Cordoba and district (areas still affected by organised Constitutional columns), Viscount Foissac-Latour with a mobile column.
6. Seville and the operations at Cadiz, Count de Boudesoulle, (commander of the I Reserve Corps), headquarters at Puerto de Santa Maria.

Four days later the Duke of Angoulême marched out of Madrid with 3,000 men. Although this left Oudinot with a weaker I Corps to protect the area, he was to be joined by the division of General Bourck once he had completed the 'pacification' of Galicia.

---

3   Those flags hidden in 1815 were only rediscovered in 1970, when they were donated to the Army Museum and again disappeared from sight into the museum's store.

5

The campaign in Catalonia, marching and counter-marching

April

Moncey's corps, on the Mediterranean coast, left its camps and crossed the frontier on the 18th April making for the Spanish town of Figueras, on the road to Barcelona. It contained, nominally, 21,000 infantry and over 4,000 cavalry (probably nearer 18,000 all told) and was destined to spend the entire campaign marching and counter-marching around the Spanish territory between the frontier and Barcelona trying to engage the Spanish constitutionalists who always managed to slip away from Moncey's clutches. The 'French sergeant' already mentioned, comments on the Spanish unpreparedness and on their belief that it would not come to open hostilities.

He says, "We daily expected orders to cross the frontiers, but the Spaniards did not believe that war was approaching them. Their troops that were in the neighbourhood of our advanced posts constantly told us that it would not take place; and when we marched into their territory about the middle of April, they retreated in the greatest confusion, with the usual exclamation, *No importante* – a consolatory saying, which Spanish pride applies to everything, indiscriminately. It appears that (the Spanish) General Milans had no idea of our movement, for he immediately abandoned the positions he held on the frontiers, and retired in the utmost disorder."

The Spanish constitutionalists facing this onslaught, under the overall command of General Mina seconded by Generals Milans and Llobera, and chief of staff Zorraquin, could count on about 30,000 men. Of this number less than half were regular troops of the line, the remainder being militia. Mina had responsibility for a number of fortresses in Catalonia, including La Seu D'Urgell, Figueras, Girona, Hostalric, Barcelona, Tortose, Lerida and Tarragona. The garrisons of these towns swallowed up most of his forces, which left only about six or seven thousand men, albeit the elite of his forces, to operate in the field.

Catalonia is a mountainous region, with many ranges running south from the Pyrenees, intersected by numerous rivers draining into the Mediterranean Sea. Two

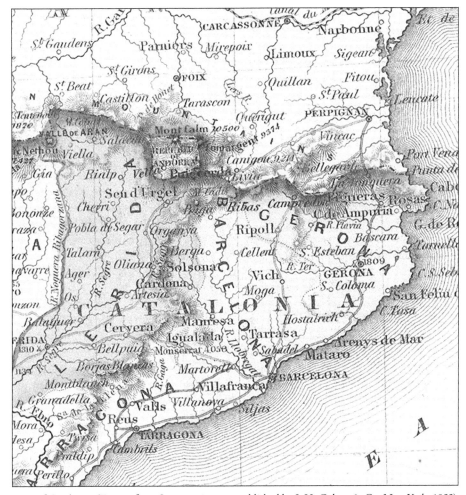

Map of Catalonia. (Extract from Spain main map, published by J. H. Colton & Co, New York, 1855)

large rivers ran west to east, the Fluvia and the Ter, the main road crossing the latter river at Girona. The road continued via Hostalric, running parallel to the coast until it reached Barcelona, the region's capital. Whilst the road ran through the coastal plain, it was bordered by steep hills which made ideal defensive positions and gave the Spanish Constitutionalists the opportunity to tie down large sections of the French army and their Spanish Royalist allies.

The first French troops to enter Catalonia were sent to occupy the Aran Valley (lying to the north west of Andorra). The Spanish constitutional militia did not dispute the French advance, but beat a hasty retreat and in scenes to be repeated all over Spain, the local populace came out to cheer the French and swear allegiance to Ferdinand and the Royalist cause.

On the 18 April, nine days after the French forces in the west had crossed the Bidasoa River, the leading elements of General Moncey's Fourth Corps, Curial's (5th) division, crossed the frontier into Catalonia. The (9th) division of General Damas followed the next day. Their first action was to invest the town of Figueras, while the brigade of Mareshal-de-camp (corresponding to Major-General) Vasserot, composed of two regiments of infantry of the Line, occupied the coastal town and citadel of Roses, where, as the fortifications were in ruins, the Spanish did not try to defend it.

On 22 April the French summoned the Spanish governor of Figueras to surrender, but he refused. However he thought it wise to evacuate the town itself and retire to the San Fernando citadel (as with many European cities Figueras retained its old fortress), which had a garrison of 2,500 men and its storerooms were well supplied. As the French entered the town they just missed the Spanish general Milans leaving with a column of about 1,200 men. He marched south to join the defending army at the river Fluvia, along the main highway to Girona. General Mina meant to oppose the French advance and brought all his forces together at Bascara, where there was a bridge over the river. The French saw an opportunity to crush the Spanish field army and the whole of the Fourth Corps was summoned to the Fluvia.

By 27 April the French were concentrated and the Marshal ordered two pontoon bridges to be constructed, one on barges and boats, and the other on trestles. As soon as the first bridge was completed two days later a French brigade and a Spanish Royalist brigade of three battalions crossed over. The following day a further French regiment crossed the river. Two brigades of the Curial division stayed on their side of the river. The 1 May was designated as the day of the general attack, but during the night of the 30 April it rained so heavily that the troop's bivouacs were flooded and roads were washed away and fords made impassable. As the French prepared to move early on the following morning they found their pontoons washed away and the attack was delayed by one day until ferries could be brought up so that the troops could cross over.

The determination of the French to force the issue was enough for the Spanish not to make a stand and they withdrew inland away from Girona, pursued by the Baron d'Eroles and his Spanish Royalists. The Spanish authorities in that city, who had been suffering from the exactions of the Constitutionalists, and who had to support the local militia through forced contributions, sent a deputation to General Moncey to hurry to the city and establish Royal authority. Girona now became the main base for the Fourth Corps and became the centre of the administration for the French army and the organisation of the Royalist Spanish forces for Catalonia.

Meanwhile, the third division (10th) of the 4th Corps under General Donnadieu was covering the flank of the advance. They had to struggle through the Pyrenees in deep snow and tell off detachments to keep an eye on the various Spanish fortified towns on their route. They were reduced to just over 2,000 men plus a few hundred Spanish royalists, but that was enough to make General Mina withdraw his scattered forces before they came to blows. Donnadieu learned of the Spanish retreat from the Fluvia and redirected his column to approach Girona from the mountains.

The town of Olot lay on their route, which was occupied by a battalion of militia and some local volunteers, in all about 400 men. They formed the rearguard of General Mina's retreating army. General Donnadieu, at the head of the French column, ordered the town to be cleared so that they could continue their march. His order was transmitted to one of his staff, *chef de bataillon* (Major) Tartaret, who took the general's escort, a second lieutenant of 12 men of the 5th Chasseurs à Cheval, accompanied by a staff captain and closely followed by the leading units of the column, two companies of voltigeurs. As they entered the town, at the trot, the Spanish retreated before them and took up a position on the slope of a hill protected by stone walls that lined the road. Tartaret continued to advance, the voltigeurs, at the double, trying their best to keep up, but being left behind. The chasseurs took two volleys from the Spanish, but did not slacken their pace, and rode into the Spaniards slashing with their sabres. The Spanish troops fled, leaving a number of dead on the field and 15 prisoners, including the colonel of the militia battalion, who were led back to the French column. Officially the French horsemen suffered a corporal killed and a trooper badly wounded. General Mina withdrew his various detachments southwards, towards Hostalric and beyond. He formed a defensive line extending from Mataró on the coast, covering the two roads that led to Barcelona and on to the mountainous region around the town of Cardedeu.

May

General Mina, perhaps realising that he could not defeat the French in battle however bravely his men fought, now devised a plan of campaign to try to manoeuvre the French out of the province. He gathered his mobile forces and marched north through the mountains in the direction of the French frontier. He hoped that Moncey would be forced to follow his movements and exhaust his corps in constant countermarches. From his bases in the mountains, well stocked with supplies and munitions, he could strike into France, or at any isolated French force, or even threaten Girona, which was now the main supply base for the French and the political centre for the Spanish Royalists. The plan was not particularly successful and Mina had to keep moving through the mountains to evade the French and Spanish Royalist pursuing columns.

The troops of General Milans were left to cover the approaches to Barcelona, but the French were approaching from two directions, from Girona towards Hostalric, extending their flank to the sea at Palamós and with General Donnadieu occupying Vic and threatening to take the Spanish in flank and rear. Palamós was occupied without a shot fired on 11 May.

The Spanish now made a move to reunite their field forces by marching on Moià, but when the news reached the French, Donnadieu's division, then resting at Vic, was given orders on the 16 May to intercept them. The following day he found the Spanish, ready for battle just south of Moià, at Casteliterçol. They were formed up on a natural amphitheatre of steep wooded hills, about 3,000 men commanded by

General Antonio Rotten. Donnadieu formed his leading units in three columns, one of Spanish Royalists under General Ramagosa, the 12th Light commanded by Colonel La Poterie and the 18th Line led by Donnadieu himself. There seems to have been little preparation, the French columns stormed the hills at the point of the bayonet with the Spanish falling back from one hillside to another. The fighting lasted for four hours, and the French admitted to 'a few men and just one officer killed', while the Spanish dead numbered 100, including the colonel of the Regiment of Léon.

A few miles to the north of Barcelona stood the ancient port of Mataró. As the French advanced they detached a force of 1,800 men (two battalions of the 6th Light; one battalion of the 7th Line; four companies of the 26th Line and the 18th Chasseurs à Cheval) to garrison the city against any foray from Barcelona. The generals in Barcelona resolved to make just such a foray and assembled over 4,000 regulars; 1,200 militia; 250 cavalry and the French and Italian Volunteer Battalion of about 500 men. The Spanish forces set out at 5:00 p.m. on 23 May in a surprise move. It then split into two columns, one taking the coastal road, the other swinging inland so as to approach Mataró from the opposite side. The coastal column arrived first around 2:00 a.m. on the 24th and surprised and captured a French guard post. The sound of the firing alerted the French garrison and the 6th Light was quickly brought forward to first hold the position and then to counter-attack and recapture the guard post. After less than an hour, the Spanish realised that their attack was of no avail withdrew to reform. The second column attacked the town, which was here defended by the battalion of the 7th Line, who held their ground. The French commander, General de Vence, led a battalion of the 6th Light and attacked the flank of the Spanish column while it was engaged with the 7th Line in front. It appears that the column broke under this assault and throwing aside their packs and weapons fled back towards Barcelona. By 11:00 a.m. the affair was all over. The French admitted to only 'a few men' as casualties, while the losses to the Spanish were considerable, including many prisoners. In a rare example of inter service co-operation, in response to signals from General de Vence, two French warships which were standing off the harbour landed some men on the coast road.

General Donnadieu had left a garrison in Vic, a battalion of the 8th Line, about 400 men and a similar number of Spanish Royalists. Mina, in his marches through Catalonia, determined to capture the town to facilitate his crossing of the river Ter. On 26 May, he brought about 3,000 men and attempted to gain access to the city by climbing over the walls. The defenders, commanded by the splendidly named Colonel the Count de Salperwick (an ancient family taking its name from a small village near Calais) of the 8th Line, manned the walls and kept the Spanish at bay and received a reinforcement during the battle of a company of voltigeurs which had been out on a foraging expedition and arrived back driving a herd of cattle. During the attack, Mina's chief of staff, General Zorraquin was wounded by a musket ball to the body, although carried away from the fighting, he died the next day. He was one of the better Spanish generals and Mina felt his loss sorely.

June

Mina withdrew his beaten army and by difficult marches led them to the fortress at La Seu D'Urgell where they could rest and be resupplied. However, he could not remain long at the fort as supplies would soon be exhausted. He determined to march through the mountains and try to gain the city of Figueras, which still held out in favour of the Constitutionalists. He set out with 3,000 infantry and a few horsemen on 5 June marching in two columns. His progress was observed by Spanish Royalist detachments and by General Rottembourg commanding French troops across the frontier. With enemies gathering about him, Mina began to retrace his steps, some French battalions tried to block his road, so he took to the mountains and small paths and tracks. One of his columns became surrounded by French troops and Spanish Royalists and after a struggle surrendered. Mina, with the remnants of his command marched on through the mountains, across French territory to the Spanish enclave of Llivia, endeavoring to regain Spain and being harassed by French regulars and National Guards. Eventually his troops dispersed and attempted to get back to safety, many falling into the hands of their enemies. Mina, after removing the insignia of his rank, finally made it back to La Seu D'Urgell with just a couple of companions, to be followed by 400 to 500 men of his shattered army. After a short rest, he and a number of volunteers again took to mountain paths, this time southwards and finally appeared at the gates of Barcelona.

July

Events now centered on the ancient city of Barcelona, reputedly founded by the Carthaginians, or it may have even existed before their arrival in the peninsula. It was occupied by the Romans and then repeatedly captured, sacked, burned and destroyed by every invader of Spain up to and including Napoleon. The local Catalans however, seemed to have survived and rebuilt and repaired their city after every 'destruction', which may explain their fierce determination for the city's continued independence. In 1820 it was one of the centres of the Spanish 'Liberal' revolution and provided support with men, money, industry and trade, the harbour providing shelter to the many privateers who scoured the sea and terrorised French maritime trade.

In 1823 the garrison, commanded by General Antonio Rotten, numbered at least 10,000 regulars supported by local militia. After the destruction of Mina's forces, there were no longer any Spanish Constitutionalists in the field, only those shut up in the fortress of Figueras and Hostalric and La Seu D'Urgell. Moncey organised his three divisions for what looked to be a prolonged siege. General Damas' division would continue with the blockade of the Spanish fortresses and on the 8 July, the divisions of Generals Curial and Donnadieu moved to invest Barcelona and its defences. Mina, was sheltering within the city and took no part in its defence due to illness and a wound he had received during his expedition, but his two subordinates, Generals Milans and Llobera, determined not to let the French have things all their own way.

The two Spanish generals took shelter behind the Llobregat River, which flowed out into the sea just to the south of Barcelona, with the object of taking the French troops forming the blockade in flank and rear. Milans, with seven battalions, was at the bridge at Molins de Rei (Molinas del Rey) and Llobera, with four battalions, further upstream at Martorell. The bridge at Martorell was cut and a strong point was established which dominated the approach to the bridge at Molins de Rei. The French decided not to wait to be attacked, but to take the initiative themselves. General Donnadieu, who was in position to the north of Barcelona, on the 9 July was ordered to attack the Constitutionalists positions.

One regiment, the 18th Line, marched on Martorell while the 3rd Line together with a regiment of hussars and a regiment of chasseurs took the river road to Molins de Rei. The Spanish made a determined resistance at the bridge, but after taking considerable casualties the French captured the bridge and cleared the strongpoint at the point of the bayonet, Milans falling back into the mountains that bordered the river valley. The 18th Line, after realising that they would not be able to cross the river at Martorell, as the bridge was broken, turned round and crossed at Molins de Rei and redirected their march on Martorell from the right bank of the river. Llobera was also forced to retreat and both generals fell back on Vilafranca. Moncey arrived with support in the shape of the 1st Light, by which time the fighting was at an end. He felt that the Constitutionalists were no longer an immediate threat to the blockade of Barcelona and ordered all the troops back to their positions around the city. The French admitted to 'considerable' casualties, no figures mentioned, but claimed to have inflicted over 500 Spanish killed or wounded.

As the battle progressed, the commander of the city, General Rotten, ordered a sortie to distract the French. Some confused skirmishing took place in the vineyards and broken country, before the Spanish retired. Nothing daunted, Rotten ordered another sortie the following day with two thousand men and four cannons. Again after several hours skirmishing the Spanish withdrew behind their fortifications. The Spanish planned a larger demonstration and in the early hours of the 13th two columns set out from the city, one remained within the protection of the city's artillery, while the other attempted to take the village of Gracia close to the walls. Again protracted skirmishing took place before the two columns retraced their steps.

August 14 to 23

In August the Constitutional forces under the command of Generals Milans and Lloberas, taking some troops from other fortresses which increased their strength to about 6,000 men, planned a fresh attempt to dislodge the French from Catalonia and relieve Barcelona, now under close siege. The main route from the French bases at Perpignan to Barcelona, ran then, as now, along the highway via Figueras and Girona and then along the coast to Barcelona. The main Spanish army had retreated within the fortifications of Tarragona, the object now was to march north towards the frontier, turn eastwards to the coast and take the town of Figueras, thus breaking the French line of communications. The march was to take in the towns of Calaf and on to Vique, (Vich) now Vic. The French were not unaware of these movements and hurried reinforcements to block the route.

On 14 August, General Milans had posted a rear-guard covering the bridge at Cabriana which was attacked by the Spanish Royalists under Baron d'Eroles, who were, however, checked by a cavalry charge. The baron, with his ADCs and an escort of ten Chasseurs à Cheval was in imminent danger of being either killed or captured when, fortuitously, two French squadrons arrived, one from the 6th Hussars and the other from the 18th Chasseurs à Cheval, which halted the Constitutionalists and forced them back. The counter charge was led by Squadron chief Martin with two platoons of hussars, just 35 men. The Royalists pursued their enemies along the road to the village of Caldes where the Constitutionalists made a stand. This village, built on the slopes of a mountain, was a natural defensive position, with the troops arranged in a semi-circle on the high ground. In front of the position was a small wood which was filled with skirmishers. D'Eroles tried to force the wood, which he did successfully, but could make no headway against the main defensive line, which consisted of the Fernando VII, Toro and Canaries regiments. General Tromelin's brigade (3rd Brigade, 11th Division, 5th Corps) arrived in support of the Royalists with the 16th Infantry of the Line deploying to the right of the enemy line, supported by three squadrons of the 6th Hussars with two battalions of the 60th Infantry of the Line facing the enemy's left.

The 16th was formed into three columns for the attack, which was matched by the Spanish, the two forces halted within musket range, deployed into line and exchanged fire, the French bringing up two mountain guns to add to the weight of fire. The Spanish infantry regiment Canaries, turned the flank of the 16th and attacked them from the rear. The French fell back suffering 8 officers and 80 men casualties including their colonel and lieutenant-colonel. The 1st Battalion of the 16th Line, under its *chef de battalion* Bonne, executed a half turn and delivered a bayonet attack which stopped the Spanish in their tracks. The Canaries Regiment was thrown back to its original position. Just at this time, at the other end of the French line of battle, the 60th Regiment was given the order to advance. It was led by the 1st Battalion under its temporary commander, Grenadier Captain Minard with the voltigeur company acting as a skirmish line. The battalion went forward up the slope, capturing a farm that the Spanish were hoping would slow them down and continued to the top of the slope and beyond that to even higher ground.

The Spanish did not make any further stand but fell back along the road to Moià. The Spanish were saved from total rout as the French cavalry could not pursue due to the nature of the ground, woods, vineyards, stone walls and mountainous terrain. The roads leading north and east were covered by French columns which determined Milans to attempt to regain Tarragona. He first marched north through the mountains, then swung west and later south, evading the French and eventually, by the 23 August, arrived back where he had set out on his expedition. The Spanish losses had been high, up to 600 men killed in action and a further 1,800 lost by desertion on the retreat to Tarragona. The French and Spanish Royalists had also suffered about 400 killed and wounded.

End of August and early September

With the Constitutionalists back within the fortress of Tarragona, Moncey moved his headquarters to Vilafranca del Penedès, so that he could keep an eye on the two troublesome generals and watch over the blockade of Barcelona. The rest of the Constitutional troops were still bottled up in Figueras, Hostalric and La Seu D'Urgell. The Spanish remained undaunted and at a council of war held in Barcelona on 28 August, resolved to send out an expedition of 2-3,000 men, and by devious routes make for Figueras, unite with the garrison and threaten the French line of communication. General Rotten chose Brigadier General Fernandez to the command of the expedition. It was formed of volunteers from the garrison and at its head marched the 'Foreign Liberal Legion' of French and Italian 'defectors' under Colonel Piechiarotti. A provisional battalion of regulars from the Leon and Ballesteros regiments followed and the column was completed with the 'Constitution' battalion, the 'National Sovereign' battalion, and a detachment of militia and 50 lancers.

On the night of the 9/10 September the troops slipped out of Barcelona and carried in fishing boats landed a few miles up the coast. They slipped inland, avoiding the French troops at Hostalric and Vic and headed for Olot on the river Fluvia. It became clear to the French General de Damas, senior officer of the district, that the Spanish were making for Figueras. Gathering what troops he could muster Damas marched with 1,100 French, 600 Royalist Spanish and 60 cavalry. Fernandez reached a village close to the fort at Figueras, but try as he might he was blocked at every turn by French infantry, cavalry and Spanish Royalists. A last attempt to gain the fort was also frustrated by French musket fire, Fernandez was wounded and his army began to break up in disorder. One of his units surrendered to the French, and this brought about the capitulation of the whole force. Two thousand men were sent prisoners to France and up to 600 killed and wounded, included Colonel Piechiarotti who had taken a bullet in the arm and later died from his wound. The garrison of Figueras had taken no part in the action just beyond their walls and eight days later surrendered. The garrison counted 1,500 able bodied men but also a further 800 sick in the hospitals and with food for only another 20 days.

General Rotten ordered yet another sortie for the 12 August to distract the French from Fernandez' mission. A force of 6,000 infantry, supported by 100 cavalry and six guns. While this was meant to be a diversion it also had the object of attempting to capture or destroy the large stores of food the French had assembled and the reserve artillery park. The action commenced before first light about 5:30 a.m. and after several hours of maneuvering and attacks the Spanish finally fell back into the city, without achieving their aims.

The Spanish strategy of maintaining their fortresses had worked well, the French did not have enough troops to closely besiege these strongpoints and hold the rest of the province. When the Spanish sent expeditions through the country and even across the frontier into France, Moncey had to continually divide his command and march and countermarch to keep contact with them. True, the country was difficult with mountain ranges and rivers and few main roads, but the Constitutionalists seemed able to go wherever they desired. Although Barcelona and the larger towns supported the Constitution, the populations of the smaller villages were generally in favour of the king and the Royalist regency which proved a disappointment and was one of the reasons that eventually led to the failure of the revolutionary government. It is also clear from the history of the campaign in Catalonia of the lack of co-operation between the various provincial Spanish armies. Other Spanish Constitutionalist forces existed across the country, but they never acted in concert with each other to bring an overwhelming force together.

Late September and conclusion of the campaign

The troops of both sides undertook little offensive action for the next couple of weeks. The French strengthened their blockades on La Seu D'Urgell, Hostalric, Barcelona and Tarragona. From this latter fortress, on 29 September, an expedition of 2,000 men set out into the surrounding countryside. The French had to hurriedly bring troops from further afield to attempt to cut off the Spanish from regaining the fortress, but only managed to find the rearguard which was engaged, inflicting a few casualties before it reached the safety of the walls of Tarragona.

On 7 October the French commander was given the news that Cadiz had fallen, the king had been released and the liberal dominated Cortez had been dissolved. The following day he sent a messenger to Generals Rotten and Mina in Barcelona with the news. They could not at first believe it and told the people and garrison that this was news from the enemy and was not to be trusted. A few days later a French general officer was sent to the fortress with the demand that the garrison hand over the city to King Ferdinand. Rotten refused the officer entry and demanded that the summons be delivered by a Spanish officer. In the meantime he sent out a battalion in a further sortie, to show that he was not to be overawed.

A council of war was held in the city with Rotten, Mina and other political leaders admitting the hopelessness of their position, but resolved to persist in their oath to defend the Constitution to the death. Moncey's only option was to turn the blockade of Barcelona into a proper siege. Heavy guns and ammunition were brought forward and gabions and fascines were constructed. These preparations seemed to have the desired effect and on 21 October an armistice came into effect to allow representatives from Barcelona to travel to Madrid to take instructions from the royal government. The armistice was to extend to Tarragona and Hostalric, but not La Seu D'Urgell which had been subject to a direct assault and had fallen on 20 October. A capitulation was agreed on 2 November and the three remaining Constitutional garrisons surrendered on the 4 November ending the Catalonian campaign.

Moncey had been given the task of pacifying Catalonia and had spent six months either blockading fortresses or chasing Spanish columns around the countryside. His own corps was never strong enough to accomplish his aims, even with the collection of Spanish Royalists who acted as his allies or auxiliaries. The Spanish Constitutionalists had probably put as many men into the field, but had split them up in small garrisons and random columns with little or no overall plan. The Spanish however seemed to have held the initiative throughout the campaign, coming and going, making sorties from their secure bases almost at will. Their mistake was to face the French in pitched battles, where better training and discipline usually won the day.

6

Molitor, From North to South

Once the French had established themselves on Spanish soil and they became aware of the defence the Constitutional armies were capable of performing, the Duke of Angoulême and his staff formed their plan. With Madrid as their goal, the main force of the I Corps and the Reserve Corps marched through northern Spain, while Moncey's IV Corps was to occupy Catalonia. The III Corps under the Prince of Hohenlohe was designated to blockade the Spanish fortresses of San Sebastian and Pamplona. General Bourck's division of the I Corps remained in the north with the object of clearing the province of Galicia and taking the important fortresses and ports of La Coruna and Vigo, where the Constitutionalists received support from abroad and Spanish privateers could find refuge. This left a large gap between the main army and the French entering Catalonia. A Spanish army under General Ballesteros operated in this gap with the ability to strike either east or west. The Duke of Angoulême detached General Molitor and the II Corps to cover Ballesteros and to neutralise the threat of his army. He was to extend his corps eastwards and link up with Moncey's troops. However as Molitor advanced and Ballesteros fell back this no longer became important.

On 26 April Molitor entered the city of Zaragoza. He established his headquarters in the city with the intention of forming the left wing of the French army in its advance on Madrid. It was assumed that Ballesteros would fall back in the direction of the capital to help protect it and that Molitor's corps would cover him. However, the Spanish general did not act as expected; he first appeared to be moving towards Catalonia, but later changed direction and began a march to the south into the province of Valencia. The French divisions had become separated as they chased Constitutional columns and ousted garrisons from the various walled towns and Molitor had to gather them back around his main base.

The division of General Pamphile-Lacroix returned from Catalonia to Zaragoza, however one of its brigades, that of Count d'Arband-Jouques marching to the river Cinca found its way impeded, on the 5 May, at the town of Monzon by some local Spanish troops, a company of regular infantry, a battalion of militia and some customs officers. A battalion of the 4th Line advanced into the town and the Spanish withdrew to an old castle situated on top of a precipitous sided outcrop of rock. The outlying fortifications were taken as the Spanish artillery posted there gave the French some trouble, but the old castle could not be taken, an attempted assault on the night of 12/13 May was unsuccessful, and it had to be bypassed, but subject to a blockade. (In 1814 this castle was occupied by a garrison of 90 French gendarmes, who had been overlooked in the general retreat of the French Imperial army and who had held out for four months until they were given proof that the French army had indeed evacuated the country.)

General Pamphile-Lacroix and his colleague General Loverdo, both had a number of skirmishes on their march and had to detach troops to watch Constitutional troops occupying forts that could not be quickly taken.

At the end of May General Molitor left Zaragoza by taking the road to Valencia, but slowly and carefully, still with an eye on crossing the mountains into Catalonia and cooperating with Moncey if needed. When it eventually became clear that although the Spanish army under Mina still presented a threat, it was only within that province and had little effect in the rest of Spain. He marched to Teruel, but made slow progress because of the bad state of the road. His engineers had to repair and remake the road, using gangs of local villagers, so that his artillery could keep up with the column. On the 8 June Molitor's divisions concentrated round Teruel.

Ballesteros had fallen back towards the city Valencia, capital of the district of the same name, but on the way found a Royalist force had taken control of the town of Sagunto (an ancient settlement, known in Carthaginian times as Arse, to the Romans as Saguntum and to the Moors as Murviedro, in 1823 it was still shown on maps as Murviedro). He tried to eject the garrison, unsuccessfully, and even started building batteries intending to conduct a regular siege. Molitor received pleas for help from the small garrison, their food and ammunition being all but exhausted. Only Loverdo's division was immediately available, and he was ordered to make all speed to prevent the fall of the town. The advance guard led by General Bonnemains, light infantry and light cavalry, was enough to make Ballesteros raise the siege, abandon his heavy artillery and head south to the river Jucar and made a stand at Alzira.

The bridge across the Jucar at Alzira was defended by over 1,000 infantry supported by some dragoons and a section of artillery. The Spanish had broken the sluices which regulated the water level in the irrigation ditches around the town, which made the river too deep to ford. The French established themselves near the bridge and attempted to repair the sluices. The two sides kept up a heavy fire for several hours, before the French finally made a desperate attempt to carry the bridge by a direct assault. The Spanish cavalry tried to dispute the advance, but gave way before the rush of the French light infantry and mounted chasseurs.

The Spanish army under Ballesteros continued its southward march, leaving the province of Valencia and entered the province of Murcia. The French continued their reciprocal advance and by 30 June arrived at Alicante. The Spanish shut the gates and the defences were too strong for the city to be taken by direct assault. Molitor had to further deplete his army by leaving a corps of observation to contain the garrison of 2,500 men. The French now halted their advance, firstly to recuperate after such a long march and secondly to give time for the convoy containing the soldiers' pay to catch them up. A seemingly minor point, but as the policy of the French was to keep the inhabitants of the districts they passed through as friendly as possible, by paying on the nail for all goods obtained locally, it was vitally important that local quarter-masters and even individual soldiers had ready cash in their pockets.

The new movement began on 7 July, Molitor arranging his divisions with Loverdo as the advance gourd, followed by Pelleport's division (who had replaced Pamphile-Lacroix as divisional commander) and followed up by General Domon with a brigade of his Dragoon division. A brigade of infantry and the second brigade of the Dragoon division remained to cover the Spanish occupied city and port of Cartagena. The road taken by Molitor's corps was blocked by the Spanish held fortress at the town of Lorca. It was vital that the advance continue without having to call a halt and commit to a formal siege. The citadel was positioned on a rocky peak protected by stone walls and batteries which covered the approaches and with a garrison of 600 men. The commander was one of Ballesteros' supporters Brigadier Gonzales Menchaca.

The leading brigade of the II Corps, Bonnemains brigade, pushed forward the 4th Light in a frontal attack against the main gate, as the only possible means of access, the assault was led by the carabineers, the elite companies of the 4th Light. As the road was narrow it took several hours for the French to break through to the fortress and the garrison became prisoners of war. As Molitor, now reduced in strength because of the number of troops detached to cover Spanish Constitutional positions, continued his advance, he was attacked by a large cavalry force, collected by Ballesteros from his various garrisons. The French relate that the Spanish, who numbered 1,200 mounted men, were eventually defeated, but retired from the field of battle in good order, leaving many dead, wounded and prisoners, but admit that they lost many horses killed and wounded. No mention is made of losses in men.

General Ballesteros led the field army of the Constitutional troops now based on the town of Granada, which was under the overall command of General Zayas. They devised a plan to lure the whole Molitor's 2nd Corps, (3rd Division, 6th Division and 2nd Dragoon Division) into a position where he could be surrounded, or at least broken, by a ruse. Zayas sent a message to Molitor, offering to surrender Granada to the French, if they would come and take it. Ballesteros moved his troops out of Granada to a position in the mountains at Campillo de Arenas, hopefully forming a trap into which Molitor would fall. The Spanish forces numbered about 7,000 under Ballesteros, not including the garrison of Granada.

General Molitor, however, had received intelligence of the Spanish movements and instead of making straight for Granada by the highway from his position at Guadiz, marched north into the mountains with the object of attacking Ballesteros. The Spanish took up positions running north-south from the village of Capillo de Arenas, to Novalejo (Noalejo) and along the mountain chain to Santa Coloma (Colomera). On the 28 July Molitor, riding ahead of the 6th Division (1st Brigade: 8th Light Infantry, 4th and 20th Chasseurs à Cheval, 2nd Brigade: 4th and 13th Line Infantry, 3rd Brigade: 24th and 39th Line Infantry) took the road to Montejicar where he met a Spanish reconnaissance of about 100 cavalry. They halted and opened fire; the

French did not reply but immediately charged. The general's escort, 50 men of the 20th Chasseurs à Cheval, crashed into the Spanish troopers, putting them to flight, but not before killing four officers and 10 men and taking a number of prisoners.

On the French left the 3rd Division of General Loverdo, (1st Brigade: 4th Light Infantry, 10th and 19th Chasseurs à Cheval, 2nd Brigade: 1st and 11th Line Infantry, 3rd Brigade: 12th and 29th Line Infantry) advanced against the high ground and encountered a Spanish regiment of light infantry, the Aragon Regiment, which was trying to work round the French and take them from the rear. They were repulsed by the 1st and 11th Regiments and the French dispersed them into the mountains, causing them a large number of casualties.

Molitor, still leading the 6th Division, got within a couple of miles of Campillo when the condition of the road got so bad that he had to leave his artillery behind, guarded by two infantry battalions. The light cavalry of the 6th Division advanced to the village of Noalejo pushing the Spanish defenders before them, before turning north towards Campillo where they supported the voltigeur companies of the 24th and 39th Line in clearing the village. The infantry continued to successfully attack the Spanish in the difficult mountainous areas. The Spanish retreated to a mountain ridge above Campillo where they engaged in a fire fight with the French, even attempting a bayonet charge at one stage. The French general seized those regiments nearest him, as the units had become mixed up, the 4th and 8th Light and the 11th and 24th Line and launched an attack against the high ridge. The Spanish were pushed from their positions and eventually retired in complete disorder to the north, leaving many dead, numbers of prisoners and quantities of equipment behind.

The terrain forbade any pursuit, the Dragoon Division was not called upon, otherwise the Spanish losses would have been higher. The French did not use their artillery as the guns could not be brought within range and there is no record of the Spanish bringing any artillery with them.

The results of the battle were disastrous for the Constitutional army, in the next two days over 1,500 men deserted, leaving only 8,000 men to defend the whole of southern Spain and to face the French and the Spanish Royalists. Molitor moved into Granada unopposed and on the 4 August, Ballesteros became disheartened with his continual failure to defeat the French in battle and being pushed from one province to another, from the Pyrenees in the north down to Granada in the far south. His army was still intact after his latest reverse, but looking at the map there was nowhere for him to go. The Spanish general opened communications with Molitor asking for an 'accommodation', not to surrender his army, but to keep it in being under his command. After negotiations a convention was signed on 6 August. He agreed to change his allegiance from the Cortez to the Royalist Regency and that any fortresses in his jurisdiction were to open their gates to the French. In return Ballesteros and his officers would keep their ranks and privileges in the army and the troops to be paid and fed as other Royalist troops. Contemporary reaction to his change of mind was that this was not a surrender due to the military situation, but a betrayal of the cause he had sworn to defend. The troops were not so easily swayed and it was only the fact that they were hemmed in by the French that assured their compliance.

General Zayas still remained in the field, ignoring Ballesteros' call to cooperate with the French and Royalists. He withdrew his corps of about 3,000 men to cover the city of Malaga on the southern coast. Leaving a garrison of about 500 men in the city he fell back on Granada. On the 4 September the French entered Malaga.

7

Bourck in Galicia

With the bulk of the French Army concentrating before Cadiz, and Moncey fully engaged with pacifying Catalonia, General Bourck was detached to act against any Constitutional forces in the north, leaving the fortresses of Santona and San Sebastian blockaded by Hohenlohe's Corps. The Duke of Angoulême ordered the army to advance on Madrid and leaving his old headquarters at Vitoria and moving to Burgos continued south leaving General Bourck, with his 2nd Division of the 1st Corps and Huber's Brigade from the 3rd Corps, to deal with the Constitutionalist army of General Morillo in his rear. Bourck marched west to the city of Leon which he reached by the 31 May.

Huber led the advance guard into the province of the Asturias and faced Colonel Juan Lopez Campillo, who attempted to break the blockade of Santona. Campillo was another former guerrilla leader who had fought against the French and had been badly wounded in 1813. His colleague was Juan Palarea y Blanes, a member of the Cortez and a former guerrilla leader and a qualified doctor, who was later taken prisoner and sent to a fortress in France . He later escaped to England and eventually returned to Spain and fought in the Carlist War on the side of the Queen. Nothing daunted Campillo tried a second time to reach Santona, but again without success. Huber, besides the French troops of the 7th Light, two battalions of the 21st Line and two cavalry regiments, also commanded the Spanish Royalist troops of General Longa, whose real name was Francisco Tomas, and who came from the village of Longa. He was a former blacksmith and guerrilla leader who achieved the rank of general in 1813.

Bourck's army followed the retreating Spanish who crossed Galicia towards the town of Corunna (La Coruna). In mid-June, Huber's column continued to march after Campillo, permitting him no rest, scattering his soldiers, capturing his baggage and by the end of June had completely destroyed his command. He was joined by General Longa who had also scattered several units of Constitutional soldiers on his advance. On 21 June the 15th Line, under General d'Albignac, came up with Colonel Palarea, who fortified a village and garrisoned it with 1,600 men. He built barricades and cut the main road, but overnight d'Albignac sent troops by a mountain route to the rear of the village. A dawn attack broke through to the village and as Palarea fell back he was attacked by the battalion in his rear, dispersing his troops. The Spanish colonel escaped with barely 300 men.

The city of Leon was the scene of a further action as the French continued their advance and exchanged fire with the Spanish rearguard, causing some casualties and capturing a general officer. The far west of Spain contains the province of Galicia where many Constitutional forces were gathered, and the important towns of La Coruna and Vigo. The Cortes had sent General Quiroga to command in La Coruna (famous for the retreat of the British army under Sir John Moore and his victory over Marshal Soult in 1809). Quiroga brought the news that the Cortes had formed a Constitutional Regency, the consequence being that Ferdinand was removed from the throne, which put Morillo in a difficult position. He supported the Cortes when they tried to limit the powers of the king, but at heart he remained a monarchist. On the 26 June, Morillo published a proclamation stating that he no longer obeyed the orders of the Cortes while he retained command of the army and the government of Galicia. He was pressured by Quiroga to accept the authority of the Constitutional government in Cadiz and by messages from General Bourck pressing him to submit to the Royal Regency in Madrid. On 10 July Morillo and Bourck met and the Spaniard agreed to support the King's government and brought his 3,000 remaining troops over to the French. Quiroga assumed command of the Constitutional troops in Galicia and fell back to La Coruna.

General Huber, still acting as the French advance guard, advanced into Galicia along the coast road. A number of skirmishes took place on his route but he pressed on, until he reached the port of Ferrol. This fortress had a garrison of 2,000 men, who promptly changed sides and declared for the Royal Regency. Bourck arrived before La Coruna on the 15 July and immediately attacked the fortifications. Just outside the main line of fortifications the Spanish had built entrenchments on the Santa Marguerita Heights. The leading French unit, the 7th Light, did not wait for the rest of the brigade, but attacked the trenches and fortified buildings and carried them at the point of the bayonet. The investment of La Coruna took only a few days to complete.

La Coruna was a fortress of the first order; it contained a navy and artillery school, an arsenal, an armoury and a powder magazine. The French troops of the field army had no heavy artillery to conduct a siege until Bourck sent to Ferrol to bring whatever heavy guns were in that fort. Twelve heavy guns were loaded onto fishing boats and slipping past a Constitutional squadron of small brigs made their way to La Coruna to equip the siege batteries.

Quiroga decide that he could better serve the Cortes by being a free agent than by being bottled up within the fortress and sailed for the nearby port of Vigo, before taking ship to England, this being, rather surprisingly, the surest route to get to Cadiz! General Novella took over the command of the garrison. General Wilson, who had been wounded fighting in the front line also took ship, initially for Vigo, but then returned to England.

The French commenced serious operations against the fort with a heavy cannonade on the 6 and 7 August and by having a number of warships cruise off the harbour.

General Novella called his staff and the senior officers present in the city to a council on the 10 August to discuss what action to take. They could not hope to stand a siege as food and military stores were lacking. Most officers voted to submit, with only four voting to continue the defence. One of these was Juan van Halen, Novella's chief of staff, who insisted that there were sufficient resources to continue the defence. Van Halen, properly Juan Manuel Julian van Halen and Sarti, Murphy and Castaneda, whose family held titles from Italy and Flanders and counted as an ancestor Sir Frank van Halen, who joined the service of King Edward III and one of the early Knights of the Garter. He had sided with Joseph Bonaparte as king of Spain in 1808, had been a cavalry officer in Napoleon's army and had even been appointed a colonel of dragoons in the Russian army. He had been tortured by the Inquisition and had been lucky to escape with his life. However the majority vote prevailed and Novella and Bourck signed a convention on 13th August, where the garrison would pass under the command of General Morillo. As Morillo entered the city on the 21 August, fighting in Galicia came to an end, the other Constitutional fortress at Vigo have already fallen.

General Bourck left small garrisons in the fortified places in Asturias and Galicia and set out for Madrid to rejoin the main French army.

8

The Trocadero and Cadiz

The Duke of Angoulême arrived at Porta Santa Maria, the headquarters of the French army before Cadiz, on 16 August. Anxious to proceed he called a meeting on the 18 August of his senior officers. Attending were the Army commanding officer, Count Bordesoulle, the chief of the artillery General Tirlet, the chief engineer General Dode and Admiral Hamlin, commanding the naval blockading squadron. They discussed the three projects for the attack, namely the occupation of the island of Leon, the bombardment of Cadiz and the assault on the Trocadero. The decision was to give priority to capturing the Trocadero which would neutralise the heavy guns which prevented the French fleet from entering the harbour.

The Trocadero

The Spanish government had taken Ferdinand to Cadiz, which they considered safe from the French and also Spanish royalist interference. The Spanish city stood at the tip of a neck of land surrounded by the waters of the Atlantic. The only road leading to the city was relatively easy to defend, and it was deemed safe from any sudden French attack. Behind Cadiz there was a large sheltered bay and Cadiz harbour was defended by batteries on the walls of the city and on the mainland by a number of forts and batteries armed with heavy guns which deterred French ships from approaching. One of these forts, on the shore of the isthmus of the Trocadero faced directly towards the city of Cadiz itself. Any French ships attempting to bombard Cadiz from the bay, or to land troops would be open to the artillery fire from this position. Earth works, redoubts and batteries had been constructed on the landward side to protect the Trocadero fort from direct assault. The strong point, called the fort of Matagorda, had been built of large stone blocks, with a battery position commanding the bay of Cadiz and with a block house and artillery galleries and platforms. The fort had been partially destroyed after the French attack in 1810 and never fully restored. To protect Matagorda itself and the other forts on the Trocadero from an assault from the mainland, trenches and a number of batteries had been constructed and an additional defence had been made by cutting a channel some 60 metres wide across the isthmus. The channel varied in depth, at high tide up to 10 feet (three metres), but at low tide

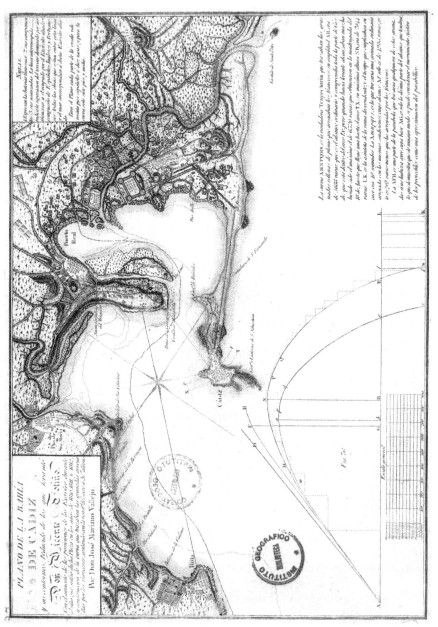

Cadiz harbour, a contemporary plate. (Open source)

little more than four feet (barely over a metre). The adjoining island of Trocadero was flat and marshy and partly covered by water at high tide and generally considered impassable by large bodies of troops. The flanks of the defences were covered by numbers of small gunboats. The line of the channel and its immediate defences had a garrison of about 2,000 men under the command of Colonel Garcés. It was also well stocked with arms and ammunition and backed up by a fortified position known as the Guerra Mill. At either end of the channel, where the Spanish considered the works most vulnerable, wooden stakes had been planted in the water, leaving a gap in the middle which was overlooked by a strong battery.

The gun positions were given names by the Spanish, those overlooking the channel, from south to north were the Batteries de Acevedo (five guns); de la Avenida (two guns); de Arco-Aguero (seven guns); de la Constitution (three guns) and de Zorraquin (four guns), all the guns of unknown calibre, as the French later removed them after capturing the defence line. The Cadiz defences in total contained more than 24 fortified posts armed with over 340 guns of various calibres ranging from 24 to eight pounder cannons, a mortar and a small number of howitzers.

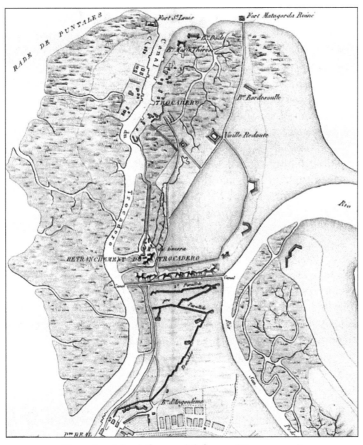

Trocadero Island, forts and defences. (Open source)

By the middle of July the French had collected a sufficient number of troops to establish a loose blockade around Cadiz. It ran from the coast at Sanlucar (de Barrameda) in the north in a rough semi-circle to Chiclana (de la Frontera) in the south close by the Isla de Leon. When the French first appeared outside Cadiz the city had barely a week's supply for the citizens and garrison. However as the blockade was but weakly enforced, especially by sea, the Spanish managed to bring in supplies from their liberal supporters, past the island of St. Peter, with its fort and powerful guns, up the canal of St. Peter and landing on the Isla de Leon, or continuing to the bay of Cadiz itself. By the time the blockade was made more effective the Spanish had amassed enough food and military stores to stand a close siege of six months.

The Sortie

As the days passed the French continued to add to their besieging army. The Spanish government in Cadiz seemed more interested in passing new laws and decrees of a revolutionary nature. Becoming more aware of their plight the Spanish mounted a sortie on 16 July which did great damage to the French preparations and boosted the confidence of the defenders. At five in the morning, about 5,000 men (some sources say 9,000, but this seems impossibly high considering the strength of the garrison.) in four columns set out from Trocadero in the north, Carraca opposite Cadiz, the bridge at San Fernando from the Isla de Leon and from the village of St. Peter. The main object of the attack was the French post at Chiclana. One casualty of the assault was Colonel Cassano of the Cadiz garrison who, at the head of his regiment of 500 men, was crossing a narrow causeway when they were fired upon by the French. The Spanish unit could not form due to the narrow ground and was driven back leaving the colonel wounded on the ground. He was taken prisoner by the French; his troops however were reformed and advanced again rescuing the colonel. Unfortunately he later died of his wounds. Both sides claimed a victory, the Spanish because they had disrupted some of the French preparations and returned safely to their starting positions, and the French who said they had forced the Spanish back behind their defences (which of course they had!).

On 28 July the French headquarters, including the Duke of Angoulême, left Madrid and made for Cadiz, taking with him the heavy guns needed if the city was to be reduced by a regular siege. However, the Duke had much to do. In those areas where the French had defeated the Spanish Constitutionalists the Royalist authorities who had resumed control were busy arresting and punishing their fellow countrymen without reference to the French military commanders, which they were obliged to do under the terms of the agreement between the two countries. No Spaniard was to be arrested without the sanction of a senior French officer and French officials were put in charge of all public newspapers. Needless to say this did not make relations between the two administrations any dearer.

On his arrival in front of Cadiz, the duke found his army to amount to around thirty thousand men. The following day he sent a staff officer to Cadiz with a letter addressed to the Spanish king. The governor of Cadiz, who was also an elected member of the Cortes, refused to let the officer talk directly to Ferdinand and promised to acquaint the king with the contents of the letter. Considering the nature of the war to date, the contents were very conciliatory in tone and asked the king, in the name of the French king, that as the insurrection was almost at an end, to treat his enemies with clemency and re-introduce to the kingdom, 'order, justice and good administration'. The King replied that he could not accept the French proposal, but would terminate the war and accept the mediation of Great Britain. The king's response was certainly written for him by members of the Cortes.

There remained nothing now for the French, but force of arms. It was decided that a direct attack on Cadiz was not feasible because the only means of attacking the city was along the narrow causeway and that the best option was to reduce the Spanish fortifications opposite the city on the Trocadero Island. This was of particular significance for the French, as during the Napoleonic war the Imperial French army had tried unsuccessfully to conquer Cadiz and the fortifications on the Trocadero. Although they had occupied the Trocadero itself they had never gained possession of Cadiz. The old soldiers saw this as a way of re-establishing their professional pride and the younger officers and those Royalists who had little military experience a means to gain a reputation and bring honour to the new French army. In purely military terms of the fortifications on the Trocadero could have been masked while the real objective of Cadiz was tackled.

Siege operations

Regular siege operations were opened on the 19 August, with trenches dug and batteries constructed. It was hard going due to the nature of the ground, low lying and soft sand overlaying hard clay and in places water at less than a metre below the surface, which could not support the weight of heavy guns without solid foundations. As well as the soft going the Spanish defenders kept up a continuous fire from their field artillery and musketry. On several occasions a sally was made by part of the garrison to disrupt the ongoing works. Work on the trenches could only be done at night as, during daylight hours, the Spanish artillery fire made it too dangerous. Spanish gunboats also added to the fire of the defenders.

On 24 August work started on a second parallel to bring the French close to the channel. On each night work was begun by up to 500 soldiers belong to the Royal Guard and the 36th of the Line. The trenches had to be wide enough to accommodate a large number of men and the countryside was scoured to bring in timber to construct gabions for the batteries and fascines to support the sides of the trench. Additionally sandbags were filled to protect the tops of the trenches and the men working in them. In his report the Chief of the Engineers of the French army, Lieutenant-General Dode de la Brunerie, stated that his men, during the operations against the Trocadero, had made up 3,600 gabions, 2,500 fascines and filled 28,000 sandbags. Under his direction over 6,000 meters of trenches were dug. A number of batteries were also constructed and with great difficulty the heavy mortars, which were mounted on naval carriages, were manhandled into their firing positions. The main batteries constructed against the Trocadero lines were *Batterie St. Louis*; *Batterie St. Charles*; *Batterie Madame* and *Batterie Monsieur*.

To encourage the men engaged in this arduous task, the Duke of Angoulême made regular visits to the works and to see for himself whether an attack was feasible. To test the proposed crossing, during the night of the 28th, Captain Petitjean of the 36th of the Line, Lieutenant Grooters of the 34th of the Line, Captain Borne of the Staff and sapper corporal Hue of the First Engineer Regiment, volunteered to test the depth of the channel. The men entered the water about 10 paces apart between the two batteries on the Spanish side where the stakes had not yet been planted. Captain Petitjean even crossed the channel to the Spanish side without being seen before returning, all the men confirming the water was shallow enough and the bed was covered in sand and that there were no obstacles in the water or on the far bank.

By 29 August the parallels were completed and on the following day an attack was made directly against the Trocadero position. A fierce cannonade was opened which lasted all day, allowing the Spaniards no respite. When the French eventually attacked by a frontal assault it was repulsed by the Spanish garrison with some loss. The Spanish were jubilant and celebrated a victory. However this was said by the French, perhaps to save face, to be only to weaken the defenders, and the real intention was to attack the following night, but in the dark hoping to find the crossing point while the tide was at its lowest and without being seen. It had been relatively easy for four men, but how would several hundred fare? This would be a difficult undertaking and the honour of leading the attack was to be given to a brigade of the Royal Guard.

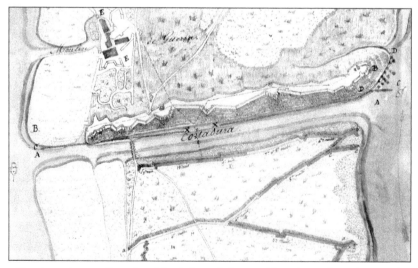

The channel across Trocadero Island, Spanish forts and French trenches. The French crossed the channel to arrive between the points marked X-X. The French sappers built the pontoon bridge to the left of the crossing. (Open source)

Attack on the Trocadero lines

Fourteen companies of elite (grenadiers and voltigeurs) infantry were formed. Those of the 3rd, 6th, and 7th (also known as the 1st Swiss) regiments of the Royal Guard formed the first column, those of the 3rd battalion of the 34th and the 3rd battalion and the 36th of the line constituted the second. The first column was accompanied by a number of Spanish Royalist infantry.

A hundred sappers and a company of artillery followed immediately behind. After these units marched three battalions made up of the centre (fusilier) companies of the Guard and the 34th of the Line with battalions of the 36th Line forming the reserve. Lieutenant-General Viscount Obert (commander of the 4th Division of the I Corps) was in charge of the attack with Baron Gougeon (brigadier commanding the 34th and 36th of the Line) leading the first column and the Count D'Escars (of the Army General Staff) the second. They had to follow the route that had been reconnoitred by Captain Petitjean a couple of nights earlier, hoping that they had estimated the low tide correctly.

On the 31 August, at 1:30 am the troops entered the trenches making sure to preserve silence. Royal Guardsman, French and Swiss, led by their Spanish allies, waded across the channel with their muskets and cartridge pouches held above their heads. However the water was deeper in places than they thought, sometimes up to the men's chests. They continued advancing through the water until they came level

The Duke of Angouleme watches the assault on the Trocadero. (Open source)

Popular contemporary print, the Guards attack across the 'channel'. (Open source)

with the embrasures of the Spanish heavy guns facing the channel. Several of the Spanish royalists clambered into the fortifications followed by the French guardsman. The Spanish garrison on that part of the line, consisting of an officer and about 40 men, exhausted by the French bombardment the previous day were found dozing at their posts. On being roused by the movement of the attackers they were reassured, in Spanish, that they were friends. A few moments later some of the garrison became aware of the large number of people in their post, they immediately called their comrades to arms and opened fire. Again the Spanish Royalists tried to calm their fears by asking why they were firing. The French did not fire back, not for any tactical reason, but because their cartridges had got wet crossing the channel. There was now complete confusion in the fortifications and the French guardsman quickly took control, the garrison being either killed or captured. The sappers continued to clear the way for the columns following and the artillerymen took charge of the guns and ensured that they were not spiked or otherwise tampered with and turned them against their former masters. The French columns now turned to right and left and attacked the redoubts and batteries from the rear sweeping the Spanish from their positions.

Charles Albert, the Prince of Carignan, future king of Sardinia, had requested permission to take part in the attack and led one of the Grenadier companies of the Royal Guard in the assault. Wading through the water he lost one of his boots, but continued to lead the grenadiers into the Spanish positions. As a mark of honour, the prince was later offered the rank of 'grenadier' in the French Royal Guard and presented with a set of red epaulettes, supposedly taken from the uniform of a guardsman who had perished in the assault. The tradition was continued when his

Another version of the French Guards attack. (Open source)

French Line infantry plunge into the water. (Open source)

son, Victor Emmanuel, king of Italy, was awarded the rank of corporal in the French 3rd Zouaves after the battle of Palestro in 1859.

Many of the Spanish artillerymen stood by their guns and were cut down. Some of the garrison did manage to escape to nearby Guerra Mill, a fortified position where some of the Spanish reserves were stationed. However, as the morning became lighter the French in overwhelming numbers quickly attacked and captured it. Some men, about 300, many of them wounded, escaped by boat across the bay to Cadiz. Fighting spread to the buildings on the island, where many of the Spanish defenders had fled. The French had to take each house by hand-to-hand fighting and suffered a number of casualties, about 70 killed, officers and men and a further 160 wounded. The Spanish lost nearly 200 men killed and 300 wounded that day as well as 40 officers and nearly 1,000 men prisoners. Among those captured was Colonel Garcias, the commander of the Trocadero forts. The French also captured 59 guns and large amounts of powder and shot. As soon as the columns had reached the opposite shore and it was clear that they had gained a foothold, a signal rocket was fired from one of the French batteries to alert the Pontoon section of the engineers who were waiting further upstream of the San Pedro river. They quickly brought up their equipment and numbers of boats scoured from the Spanish coastal villages and set about constructing a bridge across the channel. It was completed before daybreak and the returning high tide. The rest of the attacking columns could now cross dry shod and the leading companies, whose cartridges had got wet in the crossing, could be resupplied with fresh ammunition.

The Duke of Angoulême also crossed over the pontoon bridge and ordered the gun positions on the Trocadero which overlooked the bay to be repaired and new batteries built ready to bombard the city of Cadiz and the narrow strip of land leading to it.

The adventures of Sir Robert Wilson

The struggle of the Spanish Constitutionalists had much sympathy and considerable political support in Great Britain. The government adopted a neutral position, but this did not stop agitation in favour of sending some sort of help to Spain. The Foreign Enlistment Act, which prevented British citizens from joining foreign armies was in vain sought to be repealed. However, this did not stop plans being laid to send a military force. As ever cash was a problem, voices were raised in support of the Spanish revolution, but little money was contributed to the cause, about £30,000 in all. Not enough to provide an army but sufficient for a quantity of weapons and military stores.

Sir Robert Wilson, who had fought under the Duke of Wellington in Spain and Portugal against Napoleon's forces and a man of strong liberal convictions, set out for Spain followed by a number of like-minded individuals, Colonel Light, another Peninsula war veteran (later founder of the city of Adelaide in Australia); Captain Erskine; George Grenville 2nd baron Nugent (no soldier, but a Whig politician who was prepared to act on his convictions, he later went to Greece to give his support to the uprising against the Ottomans) and others.

Wilson arrived at Vigo in northern Spain with his few companions, but with no army and little military stores. The local Constitutionalists were not impressed, and with the French and their allies, the Spanish Royalists, pressing against those towns holding out against them Wilson could do little. He and his staff moved on to La Coruna which was directly under threat by the French and Spanish Royalists. During the fighting at La Coruna he fought as a simple volunteer and in trying to give some encouragement to the troops was badly wounded. He managed to get out of La Coruna and by various adventures eventually made his way to Gibraltar where he recovered sufficiently to take a further active part in the war. He evaded the French blockade of Cadiz and was given a command of part of the defences. At this point a boatload of supplies brought from England arrived in Gibraltar, was reloaded onto a local vessel and avoiding the French navy, landed within the defences of Cadiz. The English gentlemen who had brought the supplies now joined Sir Robert in defending the island of Leon, to the south of the bay of Cadiz, against the French. The list of stores brought to Spain makes interesting reading, 500 muskets and bayonets together with 50 barrels of gunpowder, much needed uniform items included 650 pairs of trousers, 630 coats, 630 waistcoats, 631 knapsacks (why the extra one is a mystery), 1,829 cartridge pouches, but only 393 pouch belts. There were also 300 canteens and a case of tools, turnscrews and worms, vital in keeping the muskets in good working order. A further transport brought more muskets and bayonets plus a few swords, 13 pistols, two rifles and one blunderbuss. Also boxes containing 50,000 flints (rumour has it that the flints were meant for cavalry pistols, so whether they fitted the muskets is open to doubt).

At the beginning of October, when it was clear that the revolution had failed, the liberal leaders and members of the Cortes who were still in Cadiz resolved not to wait for the French to enter the city, but to make their escape as quickly as possible. As soon as the Royalist government was re-established orders for the arrest of many of the Constitutionalist leaders, including Sir Robert Wilson, were made. There were a number of ships in the harbour and Wilson's companions boarded one of them bound for Gibraltar. Also in the harbour was a steam yacht belonging to the Royal Navy, HMS *Royal George*. Wilson, who at this time was a member of the Whig party and sat in the House of Commons as Member of Parliament for Southwark, sought the refuge of the Union Jack and he and his staff, which included his son, boarded the yacht which also set out for the British territory of Gibraltar. Large numbers of Spanish refugees, officers of the Constitutionalist armies and members of the Cortes all headed for the safety of British waters, where the authorities, concerned that they may bring disease with them, put the whole ragtag fleet into quarantine and forced them to fly the yellow flag. Although the refugees could not land, they could and did visit each other on board their vessels. Wilson was not yet done with Spain, in 1842, now with the rank of a Lieutenant-General in the British Army, he was posted to Gibraltar as its governor. He held the post until his death in 1849.

After the fall of the Trocadero

The French navy's entry into the bay of Cadiz was no longer impeded by the Spanish positions on the Trocadero so that warships could now be brought close in to the city walls of Cadiz and a serious bombardment could commence. The naval squadron included three ships of the line, *Le Colosse*, *Le Trident* and *Le Centaure*, six frigates and 20 canon boats with 12 bombardes and four Spanish Royalist gunboats. It took time to organise the French squadron and the first bombardment did not take place until the morning of the 23rd September. The Spanish responded with their own heavy artillery, but there was no prospect of anything except eventual destruction and defeat.

The loss of the Trocadero forts brought consternation to the Cortes and now the reality of the situation dawned on the political leaders in Cadiz. They could see no obvious way to continue the defence and on 4 September a correspondence was begun by Ferdinand, or in reality the leaders of the Cortes, and the Duke of Angoulême. The Duke responded that he would only deal with the king as a free man. Things went from bad to worse in the city, the government was beginning to run out of cash and there were signs of disaffection among the defending troops and with the commencement of the French naval bombardment things could not improve. At last the Cortes voted by 60 to 30 to abandon all further action and to allow Ferdinand to leave his captivity and join the Duke of Angoulême on the mainland. Before he left he was made to sign a declaration that all the Constitutionalists would be granted a full pardon for their actions. On the 1 October, Ferdinand and his family and suite left Cadiz and were greeted by the French leader and his staff. Needless to say Ferdinand immediately broke all the promises he had been forced to concede. His next order was to deliver Cadiz to the French army which they entered 3 October.

This marked effectively the end of the campaign, but not the end of hostilities, several fortresses still held out in favour of a now defunct Constitutionalist government. The governors of these places negotiated with the French to secure the best terms for their troops, the regulars were disbanded and the militias were to be allowed to return home unmolested by the Royalist troops. Ferdinand returned to Madrid on 13 November and immediately set about restoring his despotic government. The Duke of Angoulême retraced his steps and on 23 November re-crossed the Bidasoa River back onto French soil. By 2 December he was in Paris to receive a hero's welcome. His army did not accompany him. To guarantee Ferdinand's hold on the Spanish state, 45,000 French soldiers remained, an army of occupation in fact if not in name.

The force was organised in three divisions, one at Madrid, another on the Ebro river and a third at Cadiz.

Madrid Division

Division	Commander	Brigade	Infantry Regiment	Cavalry Regiment
Madrid	Ordonneau	Joannes		7th and 9th Chasseurs
		Clouet	23rd and 28th Line	
		Despéramont	15th and 22nd Line	

Included were one company of horse artillery and three companies of foot artillery.

Upper Ebro Division

Division	Commander	Brigade	Infantry Regiment	Cavalry Regiment
Upper Ebro	Jamin	Potier	5th Light (at Santona)	12th and 17th Chasseurs (at Tolosa)
		Higonet	3rd Light (at San Sebastian) and 6th Line (at Tolosa)	
		Quinsonas	9th Line (at Pampelune) 20th Line (at Vitoria)	

Included were four companies of foot artillery.

Cadiz Division

Division	Commander	Brigade	Infantry Regiment	Cavalry Regiment
Cadiz	Foissac-Latour	D'Hautefeuille	9th Light	13th and 14th Chasseurs
		Saporta	20th and 27th Line	
		O'Mahony	34th and 37th Line	

Included in this division were one company of horse artillery and two companies of foot artillery.

The IV Corps of Marshal Moncey was retained in Catalonia for some weeks until an occupation force was organised.

Catalonia Division

Division	Commander	Brigade	Infantry Regiment	Cavalry Regiment
Catalonia	de Maringoné	Nicolas		3rd Chasseurs and 8th Hussars
		Rapatel	19th Light and 41st Line	
		Achard	10th and 16th Line	

The district around Figueras was occupied by General Monck d'Uzer with the 40th of the Line. Also included was a field battery and two companies of mountain guns (carried in pieces by mules).

Louis XVIII wanted to honour his nephew and the Army which had performed so well in Spain and gave instructions that work on the Arc de Triumph in Paris, which had stopped in 1814 with only a third of the monument constructed, be resumed. However, instead of celebrating the French revolutionary armies and the Grande Armée of Napoleon, it was to be a monument to the Army of the Pyrenees, the army of the restored Bourbon monarchy. A new architect was appointed and plans drawn up, but little progress was made. Construction of the arch was not completed until 1836 during the reign of King Louis Philippe, when the original plans to honour Napoleon's battles and generals were fulfilled.

9

Riego's Expedition

The Spanish were not prepared to sit and await events, but determined, where they could to take the initiative. An expedition to Granada was decided upon and Riego was given the command. This province was then under the protection of the Constitutional general Ballesteros. Unknown to the leaders in Cadiz, Ballesteros had, on the 4 August, concluded an agreement with the French to put himself and his army in the service of the Royalist Regency. Riego left Cadiz on 17 August in a fishing boat and slipped past the French naval blockade, he landed at Malaga where he found 3,000 men under General Zayas. There were still a number of cities held by officers loyal to the Cortes at this time, Cartagena, governed by Torrijos, who had fought against the French invasion in 1808 and had finished the war a brigadier general at the age of only 23, and Almeria under Brigadier Guendulain.

The French, aware of the danger posed by Riego, sent General Loverdo's division of the II Corps, led by the advance guard under General Bonnemains to act against Malaga. On route he arrived at Almeria and induced Guendulain to surrender with his garrison of 700 men. However before he reached the port, a column of 400 men had left to gather 'contributions' from the surrounding area. General Bonnemains detached two companies from the 8th Light from his command to chase after this Spanish battalion. This they managed to do and forced them to lay down their arms and making prisoners of most of the Spanish.

Riego spent a couple of weeks reorganising his new army in Granada where he learned of the agreement Ballesteros had made with the French. Nothing daunted on the 2 September he marched from the city leaving a small garrison. He made for Ballesteros' camp and sought a personal interview with him to try to persuade him to change his mind and return to the Constitutionalist side. He tried flattery, offering to serve under him and when that did not succeed tried to arrest him, but Ballesteros was rescued by some of his soldiers.

As the French closed in on Riego, he slipped away towards the town of Jaen where Bonnemains caught up with him and a running fight developed, first in the town and secondly in the high ground beyond the town. The numbers were about equal with some 2,000 men in each force. The French column consisted of two regiments of light infantry and two regiments of mounted chasseurs. All the regiments were below strength, the French admitted that they had large numbers of men sick and had left

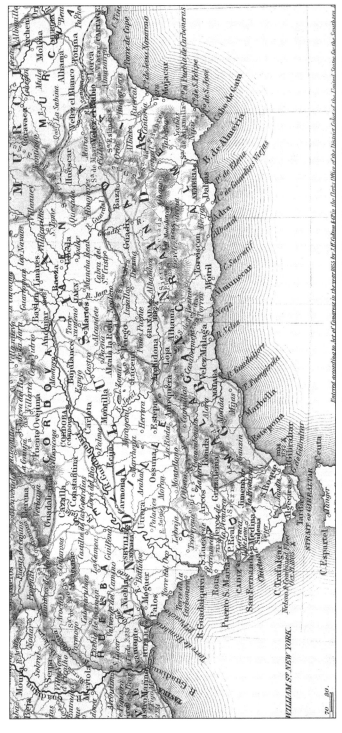

Map of southern Spain from Cadiz to Murcia. (Extract from Spain main map, published by J. H. Colton & Co, New York, 1855)

garrisons in Granada and other towns. As usual with these actions, the French sent forward their voltigeur companies to open the fighting.

Riego continued his retreat through the hills and on 13 September the French Colonel d'Argout of the Reserve Corps with three squadrons of Royal Guard Chasseurs and several companies of Guard Infantry, was sent to cut him off. On the following day near a small village, the French came unexpectedly upon Riego's rear-guard and with the element of surprise, charged, scattering one battalion of Spanish infantry and chasing the other into the nearby mountains. Riego with a few mounted companions escaped and spent the day and the following night wandering through the mountains and daybreak took refuge in a farmhouse. Here he was recognised and while he rested the local Spanish Royalists surrounded the building and broke in and arrested him. He was taken as a prisoner to Madrid to await his fate.

10

Naval Operations

Spain's lack of shipping had been a problem for the government of Ferdinand as one of his most urgent policies was to re-establish control over the American colonies. Much of the South American districts were in revolt with local armies of long established Spanish settlers and the native population coming together to remove European control. With the help of numbers of ex-soldiers now made unemployed after the Napoleonic wars, the South and Central American colonies had successfully established their independence and directed their markets away from Spain particularly towards Great Britain.

Ferdinand demanded of his ministers that troops be sent to South America to aid the Royalists still fighting against the armies of Bolívar and San Martin. While troops were being assembled, particularly around Cadiz, transport and protection for the sea voyage was lacking. Five Third Rate line of battle ships (of 74 guns) were bought from Russia, but they were of very poor quality. The problem was that the Russians used pine for their ships, which did not last long under sailing conditions and the two decks of the 74-gun ships, which were used by all the European navies, did not have as great an inherent strength as the larger three-deckers, the First and Second Rate line of battle ships. The five Russian vessels, built between 1810 and 1813, were all struck from the Spanish naval strength by 1823. Ten years seems to be about the life span of Russian warships, a large Russian frigate (carrying between 40 and 50 guns) built in 1816 and named *Patricia*, was sold to Spain the following year and renamed, *Maria Isobel*. In 1818 she escorted a convoy to the coast of Peru, where she was taken by the Chilean navy and renamed *O'Higgins* (in honour of Bernardo O'Higgins, the Chilean head of state) and became the flagship of the Chilean fleet. Unfortunately in 1823 President Bernardo O'Higgins was deposed and the ship's name reverted to *Maria Isobel*. Three years later the ship was sold to Argentina and was given the name *Buenos Aires*. Later that year she sank rounding Cape Horn.

Many smaller ships remained to the Spanish navy, gunboats, sloops and armed merchant ships to worry the French military. Indeed, some enterprising Spanish captains used their small ships in what the French considered to be acts of piracy, but to the Spanish as legitimate actions. Numbers of gunboats operated in the defence of Cadiz harbour. The French government, maintaining the fiction that they were not at war with Spain, did not issue any letters of marque to their merchant ships to act as commerce raiders. By contrast Spanish gunboats preyed on French coastal shipping. *Nile's Register*, a paper published in Baltimore (edition of 5 July 1823) prints the news that Spanish privateers were being fitted out at the port of La Coruna, in northern Spain and that a French ship loaded with cochineal (used to make a very expensive red dye) had been taken at sea and sent to Cadiz. The same paper also reports that, 'Two or three Spanish privateers have been captured by the French, whose commerce in the Mediterranean is nearly destroyed by the multitude of them afloat'.

No major battles took place at sea, but many small actions as were dictated by local events. The French troops of General Bourck before the town of La Coruna could make no headway against this strong fortress without heavy artillery, which they did not possess as part of the field army. However, they found in the town of Ferrol, a few miles away, a dozen Spanish heavy guns which would make ideal material for the batteries that were being constructed. Transport for such pieces was a problem over the poor roads in the area and instructions were given to send them by sea, across the Bay of Betanzos. Captain Fromentin of the French navy was given the task of moving the guns. He gathered together 12 local fishing boats and put one heavy gun on board each. However as the flotilla approached the bay the French spotted three Spanish brigs each armed with 18 guns. They tried to look like a fishing fleet heading out to sea, but the Constitutionalists suspected there was something untoward happening and opened fire with canister. The French managed to escape unscathed and the guns were delivered to the batteries at La Coruna.

By contrast the French mobilised a large fleet which operated in the Mediterranean Sea against the small privateers and in support of troops on the coast and to blockade cities and ports, such as Barcelona, which were held by the Spanish Constitutionalists. Numbers of larger vessels, including ships of the line operated in the Atlantic, attempting to restrict supplies reaching Spain and forming the blockade against the last Spanish capital of Cadiz.

In 1822 the French navy had 246 vessels of all kinds on the books, including 46 ships of the line (battleships carrying various numbers of guns, First, Second and Third rates with upwards of 70 arranged in broadsides) and 34 frigates (again of various sizes with batteries of 18 to 32 guns). However, because of financial constraints only 84 vessels were to be armed, including three battleships and 12 frigates. The fleet assembled under Rear-Admiral Hamelin eventually totalled 67 ships, all three ships of the line and the 12 frigates, plus a further frigate which was put into service. No sooner was the fleet ready to sail when Hamelin fell ill and was replaced by Rear-Admiral Duperre, an experienced sailor who had won a notable victory against the Royal Navy in 1810 at Mauritius.

The largest ship was the *Centaure* of 80 guns, which was stationed off Barcelona and later moved to join the fleet opposite Cadiz. Also opposite Cadiz were the *Colosse* and the *Trident*, both 74-gun ships of the line. They were supported by a number of frigates, the largest the *Venus* of 24 guns and eight smaller frigates of 18 guns. A further 15 vessels including corvettes, brigs, and gunboats also formed part of the fleet. Duperre closed in on Cadiz with his largest ships reducing any Spanish fortifications that could embarrass the French. They started with the Isle Verte in the bay of Algeciras (opposite Gibraltar), which was reduced on 13 August, after a long bombardment. They worked round the coast towards Cadiz, coming to the island of St. Peter which eventually fell on 20 September after putting up a strong resistance. Admiral Duperre's report on the capture of St. Peter states that his ships opened a sustained bombardment for over an hour, with the fort responding, but could not match the rapidity of the French fire. At half past three in the afternoon, Duperre ordered that launches be prepared to carry 420 infantrymen from the 12th and 24th Line (drawn from Molitor's 2nd Corps) and a detachment of grenadiers from the naval artillery to take the fort, when a white flag appeared on the wall of the fort. As the troops landed they were met by a Spanish officer who was conveyed to the French admiral to request terms for surrender. Terms were agreed, but most of the garrison preferred to become prisoners. The French found 27 bronze 24 pounder guns, large stores of ammunition and food for two months. Of the garrison of 180 men, 13 had been killed or wounded. The French losses were slight, only a few wounded, the largest French ship the *Centaure*, had no casualties, most of the Spanish missiles flying high and only causing damage to the rigging.

The fleet was now in a position to bring the fire of its heavy guns against Cadiz itself.

The frigate *Maria-Therese*, 24 guns, operated against Barcelona, in company with 15 smaller ships. Nine small vessels supported the troops in the northern provinces, cruising the Bay of Biscay.

The legal niceties were observed and notification was sent to the ambassadors and ministers of neutral powers by the French Minister of Foreign Affairs that, on 28 July, a blockade was declared against the ports of Cadiz, Barcelona, Santona and St. Sebastian. A later note, on 5 August, added the port of La Coruna to the blockade.

Other nations took active steps to keep from becoming embroiled in any diplomatic problems with France, and maintaining strict neutrality, the King of the Netherlands published a decree on the 21 April prohibiting the fitting out of privateers under the French or Spanish flags, in Holland or any of its colonies.

In honour of the conduct of the master and crew of the *Centaure* during the campaign, on 12 October the king signed an ordinance renaming the ship as the *Santi-Petri*.

11

Fortresses

One of the interesting and unusual aspects of the campaign was the number of fortresses in the Iberian Peninsula that the Constitutionalists used as pivots to support their armies in the field. Large sums of money and great efforts had been made to repair or build new forts, castles and citadels in every province. Most, if not all, had been used during the Napoleonic invasion and subsequent war from 1808 to 1814, by both sides. Some of these strong points were based on medieval fortifications strengthened by modern artillery, others modern constructions. Cadiz was a walled city protected by coastal batteries and outlying forts. Barcelona was another walled city but with a separate citadel, essentially a fort within a fort. Other towns contained a citadel which could be defended even though the town it was connected to was occupied by an enemy.

In many cases during the French advance they bypassed many Spanish strong-points leaving a greater or lesser blockade to neutralise any offensive action by the garrison. The problem for the French was a lack of men to conduct a proper siege and in some cases a lack of heavy artillery to batter down enough of the fortress to make a practicable breach. One method of capturing a fortified position was to starve out the garrison, but this depended on a tight blockade. Some Spanish posts had enough in store to stand a long siege, others could get resupplied by various means. Cadiz, when first approached by the French army had only enough food and materials of war to last a couple of weeks, but by the time of the battle of the Trocadero, they had restocked their magazines to last for several months.

While the tactic of bypassing and covering enemy strongpoints was well founded, it had after all been used by the Allied armies invading France in 1814, it did require a large number of men and a strong force of artillery.

The result was that as the campaign progressed and the French occupied more and more of Spain, they were leaving large numbers of their troops to besiege, or blockade or cover Constitutionalist held positions. The army of a 'Hundred Thousand Sons of St Louis' which had crossed the frontier in April was reduced to around 30,000 men for the siege of Cadiz in August.

Moncey, in Catalonia, spent much of his time marching back and forth between fortified cities and chasing small columns of Spanish troops as they emerged from one fortress or another. In the north the III Corps under Prince Hohenlohe was given the task of covering three large Spanish fortresses, Santona, San Sebastian and Pamplona. The whole of the French 7th Division together with the Spanish Royalist division of Count d'Espagne were employed to blockade Pamplona, a brigade was used to contain San Sebastian and another to watch Santona.

Pamplona

Pamplona is the capital of the province of Navarre and as such a large city which had a strong curtain of walls and a large fortress attached to the south of the city, some of which still survives. By mid-May the investment was complete. All did not go according to plan as in June the Spanish Royalist division supporting the French besiegers became disaffected and the Volunteers of Navarre who formed the majority of the troops decided to take the division's treasury and march off! On 18 July the garrison executed a sortie with over 1,000 men, supported by artillery. Their attack was principally directed against the Spanish Royalists, the infantry regiment of Don Carlos, which fell back before the onslaught only to be rescued by a battalion of the 3rd Light.

A change of command in late August also altered the conduct of the siege. Marshal Lauriston arrived on 27 August and asked his engineer officers to prepare a plan for an assault. He proposed a regular attack with trenches, saps and batteries against the citadel. As a diversion an attack was launched, on the 8 September and kept up on the following day, against a suburb of the city which lay outside the walls and on the opposite side to the citadel. This hopefully would keep the Spanish attention away from the real point to be attacked. Starting on the 10 September work began on the trenches and continued until the 15 September, and at daybreak on the following day the artillery in the siege batteries began a bombardment against the Spanish artillery positions which were gradually demolished. By 2:00 p.m. the Spanish guns ceased to fire and a white flag was displayed on the ramparts. The next day the two sides met and terms for surrender were agreed. The French marched into the city and the garrison of 3,800 were sent as prisoners of war back to France.

Santona

Halfway between the cities of Bilbao and Santander on the Biscay coast of Spain sits the small town of Santona. What makes this town significant is its large and secure harbour. It was a base for the Spanish navy as it had a large entrance and a deep water anchorage. The Constitutionalist garrison was quite large, large enough to send out, on 2 July, a force of five to 600 men in boats to harass the French camps inland. They made some progress against two companies of the French 35th Line and one company of the 21st before the village of Colindres until they were counterattacked in flank by another company of the 21st coming from the town of Laredo. The Spanish returned to their boats and headed back to their base. The French also made harassing attacks and on the night of 21 August Captain Dast made an attack on a forward post with a company drawn from the 5th Light. It took the post, killed some the garrison and retired with five prisoners. The French were not immune from the forts' artillery, a small gunboat, on a reconnaissance of the harbour took an unlucky shell in its powder magazine and blew up killing several staff officers. As the military and political situation worsened for the Spanish, the governor of Santona surrendered to the French on 28 September.

San Sebastian

Barely 12 miles (20km) from the frontier the city of San Sebastian had become the refuge of many of the Constitutional units who fell back from the initial French invasion. It is situated on the coast and the garrison under Colonel Carlos O'Donnell, felt confident that they could hold out with supplies sent by sea. At first the French merely set up a blockade on the landward side. On 15 July the garrison made a sortie to clear some of the houses in front of the town. After setting some on fire they began to withdraw, the French following them closely trying to douse the flames. Thereafter the French were satisfied to keep up the blockade and the Spanish to sit tight and await events elsewhere. Eventually, on the 3 October, with the fall of the Cortes government, the garrison surrendered.

12

French uniforms

The Royal Guard

With the first Bourbon restoration in 1814, the old royal guard was reformed, the disposed nobility retuning, expecting to get back their former ranks and privileges. Some of the resurrected formations did not long survive the second restoration, after Napoleon's final defeat at Waterloo, the expense of maintaining the 'Musketiers' for example, proved just too great for the French treasury. The *Cent Suisse, Gardes de la manche, Les gardes de la porte, Le Garde de la prevote de l'hotel* all went the same way, although some, such as the last named, were replaced as police of the royal residences, by a company of Elite Gendarmes.

The *Cent Suisse* became the company of 'King's Ordinary Foot Guards'. The uniform for this guard company was; a royal blue tail coat with red collar, cuffs, cuff flaps and turn backs, gold grenade badge on either side of the collar and on the coat turn backs. The nine gold buttons on the front of the coat were decorated with broad gold lace bars as were the three buttons on each coat tail false pockets and with red piping on the pocket edge. In undress the Guard had a royal blue tailcoat with red collar and blue cuffs and turn backs all piped in red, but without the gold lace bars. In both orders of dress the Guardsmen wore yellow epaulettes with red pads and fringes of yellow mixed with gold thread. Headgear was a bearskin cap with a gold front plate bearing the royal arms, a red patch at the rear with a gold grenade, cords and

French Grenadier of a Guard regiment.
(Eugene Lami)

105

flounders of yellow mixed with gold tread and a white plume rising from a white cockade (all French troops wore a white cockade until the revolution of 1830, when it was replaced by the tricolour cockade). White trousers for summer or blue trousers piped red for winter. White cross belts supporting a black leather cartridge box and a distinctive sabre.

In 1816 the Royal household troops were replaced by a Royal Guard. It was organised as two divisions of infantry and a cavalry division. Many of the guardsmen and NCOs came from the disbanded regiments of the Napoleonic Imperial Guard, whereas many officers were 'emigrés', nobles who returned with the reestablishment of the Bourbon monarchy.

Infantry

1st Division	1st Brigade	1st Regiment of the Guard
		4th Regiment of the Guard
	2nd Brigade	2nd Regiment of the Guard
		5th Regiment of the Guard
2nd Division	3rd Brigade	3rd Regiment of the Guard
		6th Regiment of the Guard
	4th Brigade	7th (1st Swiss) Regiment of the Guard
		8th (2nd Swiss) Regiment of the Guard

Each regiment comprised three battalions, each with eight companies, one of grenadiers, one of voltigeurs and six of fusiliers, called 'ordinary' or centre companies. (see Chapter 2 for details of organisation).

Swiss and French Guards.
(Unknown artist)

Cavalry

1st Brigade	1st Regiment of Mounted Grenadiers
	2nd Regiment of Mounted Grenadiers
2nd Brigade	1st Regiment of Cuirassiers
	2nd Regiment of Cuirassiers
3rd Brigade	Regiment of Dragoons
	Regiment of Chasseurs a cheval
4th Brigade	Regiment of Lancers
	Regiment of Hussars

The guard contained its own support of eight companies of Foot Artillery and four companies of Horse Artillery and a company of Engineers.

Royal Guard infantry

The first six (French) regiments were dressed in a single breasted royal blue coatee with sort tails, closed by a row of nine silver metal buttons. The collar was also blue, but the regiments were distinguished by coloured cuffs, cuff flaps, turnbacks and piping. The two Swiss regiments had the same style of coatees, but of scarlet cloth.

Regiment	Collar	cuffs	cuff flaps	turnbacks	turnback piping
1	blue	red	blue, red piping	red	white
2	blue	dark pink	blue, dark pink piping	dark pink	white
3	blue	yellow	blue, yellow piping	yellow	white
4	blue	red	red	red	white
5	blue	dark pink	dark pink	dark pink	white
6	blue	yellow	yellow	yellow	white
7 (1 Swiss)	blue	blue	blue, red piping	white	NIL
8 (2 Swiss)	red	blue	red	white	NIL

White trousers in summer, dark blue piped in the regimental distinguishing colour in winter dress. In full dress the front of the coatee was decorated with nine white lace bars, wide enough to look like a plastron, with further lace on the button holes on the coat tails. The different companies had a white cloth badge on each of the coat turnbacks, a grenade for the grenadiers, a hunting horn for the voltigeurs and a *fleur de lis* for the fusiliers. These badges were of red cloth for the two Swiss regiments. White cross belts supporting a black leather cartridge box and a sabre and bayonet.

The guardsmen wore a bearskin cap, for the grenadiers with a yellow metal plate, patch in the distinctive facing colour with a white grenade, white cords and flounders and a white plume rising from the white cockade of the Bourbon monarchy. Voltigeur companies did not have the metal plate and had a white hunting horn badge on the facing colour patch, fusilier companies initially had a black felt shako but changed to a cap similar to the voltigeurs, but without the cords and flounders and with a white *fleur de lis* badge on the facing colour patch. Grenadiers had red epaulettes and fringes, voltigeurs green straps and red fringes and fusiliers all white epaulettes and fringes.

A grey double breasted greatcoat was worn and in undress a tailcoat without the white lace bars was issued and headgear could be a bicorne hat or a *bonnet de police* of a larger cut than the Napoleonic style.

In the two Swiss regiments, the grenadiers wore the bearskin cap with yellow metal plate and white cords and flounders, while the voltigeurs and fusiliers retained the black felt shako, the voltigeurs with white cords and flounders, the fusiliers without. White epaulettes for all companies, red crescents for grenadiers, green crescents for voltigeurs and plain white for the fusiliers.

For officers of the Royal Guard, the coatee had long coat tails and silver replaced the white lace decoration on the bearskin and the front of the coatee of the NCOs and guardsmen.

The *Compagnies Sedentaires* (Veterans companies) wore a single breasted royal blue coatee with a red collar, cuffs and turn backs and red fringed epaulettes, white metal buttons. White trousers in summer dress, blue with red piping for winter. Black shako with yellow metal plate and chinscales, white cords and a white plume. All ranks of the first company, the Company of NCOs, wore two silver lace bars on either side of the collar.

Infantry of the Line

The 60 (numbers 61 to 64 raised in February 1823) regiments of the infantry of the line, which replaced the departmental legions received a new uniform of a single breasted royal blue tailcoat with coloured collar, cuffs, turn backs and piping. It had nine yellow metal buttons down the front of the coat, three on each cuff, two in the small of the back, three on each false pocket and one on each shoulder strap. The buttons were stamped with the regimental number. There were eight groups of colours to distinguish the regiments, with different arrangements of the facings.

Regiments	Facing colour	Regiments	Facing colour
1 to 4	white	33 to 36	white
5 to 8	crimson	37 to 40	crimson
9 to 12	yellow	41 to 44	yellow
13 to 16	dark pink	45 to 48	dark pink
17 to 20	orange	49 to 52	orange
21 to 24	sky blue	53 to 56	sky blue
25 to 28	buff	57 to 60	buff
29 to 32	light green	61 to 64	light green

The table is based on the regulations dated 8 May 1822, further regulations issued on 2 February 1823 which brought in the facing colour collar tabs also changed the facing colour of regiments 29 to 32 and 61 to 64 from light green to yellow.

Regiments numbers 1 to 32 had the collar, turnbacks, cuff flaps, piping and fusilier shoulder straps in the facing colour; regiments 33 to 64 had blue collars and cuff flaps with the cuffs, turnbacks, piping and tab on the collar in the facing colour. Blue trousers piped in the regimental facing colour. A new model iron grey double breasted greatcoat was introduced with collar, or collar tab in the facing colour. The buttons of each infantry regiment and indeed each cavalry regiment carried the number of the unit within a decorative border. These decorations were different for each arm of service and also for each type of cavalry.

All the foot troops were issued with a white pull-on shirt with a single button on the collar; white draws which extended down to mid-calf with a button closed fly; a black stock with a buckle closure at the back of the neck; black (winter) and white (summer) gaiters with nine small bone buttons and a loop which extended under the shoe and black leather lace up shoes with hob nails on heel and sole. The trousers, which were issued in place of the Napoleonic breeches and gaiters, had a button opening front flap and were held up by braces over the shoulders. For undress each man had a single breasted sleeved waistcoat in the same colour as the jacket with the regimental

facing on the collar only and as a working dress the men were issued with a white version of the waistcoat. There was also a new model *bonnet de police* in blue piped in the facing colour and with a small tassel at the front. It also had a small cloth decoration of either a *fleur de lis*, a grenade or a hunting horn depending on the company.

The companies were distinguished by coloured epaulettes, red for grenadiers, yellow for voltigeurs and plain straps and pads for the fusiliers, regiments 1 to 32 in the facing colour with blue piping and regiments 33 to 64, blue with facing colour piping. A new model shako was introduced in 1822, narrower than the 1820 model it replaced. The shako had a coloured band, in the facing colour, round the top of the body. The yellow metal plate had a crowned shield with the

French corporal of fusiliers, Infantry Regiment 34, uniform regulations of 1822, in February 1823 the collar was changed by adding a small tab in the facing colour (white in this case) to the front. The rank is shown by the two white wool stripes above the cuff, the red inverted chevron on the upper arm is a long service distinction. (Author's collection)

Bourbon arms of three *fleur de lis* over an amazon shield with the regimental number as a cut out. Yellow metal chinscales. Grenadiers had a red plume and voltigeurs, yellow, fusiliers had a flattened colour disc, royal-blue for the 1st battalion of the regiment, crimson for the 2nd and yellow for the 3rd bearing a yellow metal company number on both sides. The cockade was plain white metal.

Grenadier distinctions were a grenade badge in blue cloth on the coat tail turnbacks. The voltigeur companies a blue cloth hunting horn badge; fusilier companies blue cloth *fleur de lis*.

The elite companies carried their equipment on white cross-belts, pouch on the right hip and a short sword on the left. The bayonet scabbard was attached to the belt just above the pouch. Fusiliers wore a single belt over the right shoulder supporting the pouch and bayonet. Brown cowhide pack with rolled grey greatcoat on white straps. All foot troops who were armed with a firearm had a small brass chain looped through a button hole and carrying a small 'picker' to clear any blockage of the musket touchhole.

Light infantry

The 20 regiments of Light Infantry all wore the same uniform of royal blue tail coat with blue pointed cuffs, piped yellow, yellow collar, piped blue and yellow turnbacks. The coatee had yellow piping down the front and on the rear false pockets. The arrangements of buttons were similar to the line infantry, but in white metal. Blue trou-

French fusilier in campaign dress, regimental number painted on the front of the shako cover, yellow pompon denotes the Third Battalion. The regimental facing colour, crimson, shown on coat collar. (Author's collection)

sers piped yellow, with white trousers for summer wear. The centre companies, named *chasseurs*, had a single shoulder belt to support the cartridge pouch and bayonet and *fleur de lis* badges on the coat tails. The elite companies, carabineers instead of the grenadiers in the line regiments, had white cross belts and a grenade badge on the coat tails and the voltigeurs had a hunting horn. Red epaulettes for the carabineers and yellow for the voltigeurs. Blue shoulder straps piped yellow for the chasseurs.

The shako was similar to the line infantry, with a yellow cloth band round the top, red plume for carabineers, yellow plume for voltigeurs and a flattened disc with the number of the company for the chasseur companies. White cockade, yellow metal plate and chinscales. The plate had the regiment number as a cut-out on the amazon shield within an embossed hunting horn.

On 22 May 1822, by an order of the king, the light infantry signallers had their cornets (similar to a hunting horn) replaced by a new instrument, the clarion (resembling a valveless trumpet).

The regimental sappers, continuing the traditions from the Napoleonic army, wore bearskin caps, a white leather apron and were armed with a short carbine and special sword with a saw tooth back.

The uniform for officers was similar to that of the men. However, as an officer would have his uniform made by a private tailor it would be of better quality material and with slight differences, for example some surviving examples show the cockade worn on the front of the shako to be made from white silk and the shako fittings (plate, chin-scales and band around the top) to have a gilt finish.

Swiss infantry regiments

There were four regiments, inherited from Napoleon, on the establishment recruited from the Swiss Catholic cantons. Their uniforms were of a similar style and cut to the infantry of the Line, but the basic coat colour was red. Following tradition they were named from their commanding colonels, the 1st De Bleuler; the 2nd De Freuller; the 3rd De Steigeur and the 4th De Salis. The 1st Regiment had a blue collar, turnbacks, cuffs and cuff flaps, the 2nd black collar and turnbacks and red cuffs and cuff flaps, the 3rd black collar, turnbacks, cuffs and cuff flaps and the 4th red collar cuff flaps and blue turnbacks and cuffs. All had yellow metal buttons. White trousers in summer. The blue winter wear trousers were piped in red.

Regiment de Hohenlohe

Following the 'Hundred Days' the former members of the eight foreign regiments of the French army which remained in France were reorganised as the Royal Foreign Legion. In 1816 it was renamed The Legion of Hohenlohe after its commanding officer. This formation was the forerunner of the French Foreign Legion. It wore a mid-blue coatee with yellow facings and white metal buttons befitting its light infantry role.

Medical officer of the Hohenlohe Regiment. (Unknown artist)

Colonial battalions

In 1816 the colonial battalions were dressed similarly to the departmental legions. The colour of the coatee was light grey with blue collar, cuffs and plastron, Grey breeches and black gaiters. After 1816 the Colonial troops followed the metropolitan French army style and by 1823 had adopted the single breasted coat. There existed three battalions. As an example the French colony of Guiana in South America was home to a Colonial battalion with fusilier companies dressed in a blue tailcoat with a red collar and red piping on the front of the coat and round the cuffs, shoulder straps and on the turn-backs. The grenadier company had, in addition, red fringed epaulettes, red band round the shako and a red pompon and tuft. The chasseur company had yellow piping on the collar, cuffs and coat, white metal buttons in place of the yellow metal for the rest of the battalion. The shako had white metal plate and chin-scales and a yellow pompon. Yellow piping to the turn backs, although JOB[1] shows the turn-backs completely yellow. As well as the European troops, there was also a chasseur company recruited from the local Guyanese. The Indian sepoy battalion wore a royal blue coatee with red lapels, pointed cuffs and fringed epaulettes. Blue sash round the waist and white 'shorts' edged red. Light locally made sandals. The hat was a large white 'pancake' style edged with red tape and with red tapes radiating from a central pompon.

French Sepoy. (Eugene Lami)

Discipline Companies

When the unit was formed in 1818, the four companies of fusiliers had white coatees with collar, cuffs and lapels also white, scarlet piping round all these features, with white metal buttons. The Pioneer companies had a beige coat with a royal blue collar and yellow metal buttons. At the end of 1822 both types of companies were dressed in an all royal blue coatee with red piping on the collar, cuffs and turn backs and false

1   Jacques Marie Gaston Onfroy de Bréville, French artist and illustrator, noted for the accuracy of his depictions of military uniforms.

French militarised Customs officers.
(A. de Valmont, *Costume Militaires Francais 1814-18 30*, Vol. IX)

pockets on the coat tails. Yellow metal buttons. White trousers in summer, royal blue with red piping in winter dress.

Most contemporary illustrations of French troops in action show the men in campaign dress, shako covered with a white cloth, as was the cartridge pouch. On the front of the shako cover the regimental number was painted on with black paint. The pompon was in the battalion colour, blue for the First Battalion, crimson for the Second and yellow for the Third. The double breasted greatcoat was iron-grey with yellow buttons. It had button holes on the front skirts so that it could be fixed back for marching. The collar, in the case of the 7th Regiment was solid crimson. Trousers were also iron-grey. Blanket carried on the top of the pack in a white bag with blue stripes.

Cuirassiers

The six cuirassier regiments had blue tail-coats and each had their own facing colour on the collar, cuffs, cuff flaps and turn-backs. Blue piping on the collar, cuffs and cuff flaps. The turn-backs were decorated with blue cloth grenades. As befitting elite troops the cuirassiers wore red epaulettes. The facing colours were: 1st Regiment, scarlet; 2nd, crimson; 3rd, orange; 4th, pink; 5th, yellow and 6th buff. The facing colour was also carried as edging on the blue saddle cloth. The helmet had a steel bowl, a brass crest which carried a black wool 'caterpillar'. Black fur turban and brass chin-scales and edging to the front and rear peaks. White metal buttons down the front of the tailcoat. three small buttons on the cuff flaps and on the false pockets on the coat tails. Steel cuirass with a red cloth lining edged white, brass shoulder chains. White breeches and high black boots. White gauntlets. The long straight sword was carried in a steel scabbard suspended from a white leather belt, white sword knot. The shabraque was royal blue with white edging and a white grenade in the lower corner. The round mantle roll was also blue with a piping at each end in the regimental colour. A white sheepskin with a vandyke edging also in the facing colour was used to cover the saddle and saddle bags.

Dragoons

The 10 regiments of dragoons had dark green tail-coats, the first two regiments had pink lapels and collars and cuff flaps, green epaulettes but with no fringes. The second two regiments had pink lapels and green collars, pink cuffs and green cuff flaps. Pink fringeless epaulettes. The 5th and 6th regiments had yellow collars and lapels. Green cuffs and yellow cuff flaps, green fringeless epaulettes, piped yellow. The 7th and 8th regiments had yellow lapels, with a green collar. Yellow cuffs with green cuff flaps, yellow fringeless epaulettes piped green. The 9th and 10th regiments had a red collar and lapels, green cuffs with red cuff flaps, green fringeless epaulettes piped green. Blue grey long trousers with piping on the outside seam in the facing colour. White waist belt with a brass buckle to support the sword and a white shoulder belt to carry the short carbine. The helmet was similar to that worn by the cuirassiers, but all in brass and with a brown fur turban. In all regiments the tails of the coats had a *fleur de lis* cloth badge on the outside tail and a grenade badge on the inside tail, all in the facing colour. Red saddlecloth with green edging and a green grenade badge in the lower corner. White sheepskin covering the saddle. Portmanteau green with red ends showing a green grenade badge with the regimental number in red on the 'bomb'.

Chasseurs à cheval

The mounted chasseurs made up the largest number of cavalry regiments, in 1822 the number stood at 24. In that year they were given a new uniform which looked somewhat similar to a hussar style. The whole force had a green short tailed coat with three rows of buttons connected by coloured cords. The same coloured cords connected the shako to the left shoulder of the coat and were green mixed with the facing colour. The regimental colours were, 1st, 2nd, 3rd and 4th, scarlet; 5th, 6th 7th and 8th, yellow; 9th, 10th, 11th and 12th, crimson; 13th, 14th, 15th and 16th, sky blue; 17th, 18th 19th and 20th, pink and 21st, 22nd, 23rd and 24th, orange. The first two regiments in each group had the collar in the facing colour piped green and the cuffs in green piped in the facing colour, the second two regiments had a green collar with a small patch in the facing colour and cuffs in the similar colour. The facing colour also appeared on piping to the coat tails, round the false pockets and the hunting horn badges on the coat tails. All buttons were of white metal. The chasseurs wore a tall black shako with a white cockade on the front and an 'olive' denoting the squadron (1st squadron, royal blue; 2nd, crimson; 3rd, green; 4th, sky blue; 5th, dark pink; 6th, yellow) and black plume topped in the facing colour. Brass chin-scales. Red riding overalls reinforced with black leather. White cross belts over the right shoulder supporting the short carbine and a cartridge pouch. The lance carried by the first and sixth squadrons carried a pennon of two colours, the regimental facing colour in the upper half with white below. Red saddlecloth with green edging and the regimental number in the lower corner. White sheepskin, portmanteau red with green hunting horn badge on the ends.

Hussars

There were six regiments of hussars on the French establishment. They retained the typical style of uniform with a dolman and pelisse decorated with coloured braid. In each regiment the dolman and pelisse were of the same colour. For the 1st Regiment, sky blue, the 2nd Regiment a brown-maroon, for the 3rd Regiment blue-grey, the 4th Regiment red, the 5th Regiment royal blue and the 6th Regiment green. All regiments had red trousers, apart from the 4th regiment which had sky-blue. The dolman and pelisse each had three rows of 18 white metal buttons; the buttons were decorated

French hussar.
(Unknown artist)

with loops of coloured braid, which was red with a mix of the regimental colour. The exception was again the 4th Regiment which had a mixture of red and sky-blue. All regiments wore a barrel sash of crimson and white wool. The shako was covered with red cloth, apart from the 4th having plain black. On the front of the shako a white cockade and in full dress a black plume. At the base of the plume a small pompon denoting the squadron, first squadron royal blue; second crimson; third green; fourth sky blue; fifth dark pink and sixth yellow. These were silver for officers, as were the buttons and braiding. White sheepskin saddle cover.

All mounted troops were provided with a riding coat, a sleeved cloak with a cape, riding breeches with reinforced leather inside legs, riding boots with hob nails on heels and soles and fixed spurs.

Artillery

The artillery preserved much of its Napoleonic appearance, dark blue tail coat with a blue collar and cuff flaps, all piped red, red cuffs. The lapels were blue with red piping. Dark blue trousers, white gaiters. Yellow metal buttons. Red epaulettes. White cross belts supporting a cartridge pouch and a short sword with a cross hilt. The shako was black with yellow metal plate and chin-scales, red cloth band round the top of the crown and a red wool ball and tuft. White cockade.

Artillery Train

The drivers and crews of the artillery train wore an infantry shako with white metal plate and chinscales and a red pompon. The coatee and riding trousers, or breeches, were termed 'iron-grey' a shade of mid blue, with royal blue collar, round cuffs and cuff flaps, turn backs and piping. White metal buttons.

The uniform of the medical companies was in the style of the light infantry, basic colour was grey with piping of a browny-maroon colour, buttons of white metal. Shako as the light infantry.

The two military schools had their own uniform, based on the infantry model. St. Cyr had a royal blue coatee with red collar, round cuffs, turnbacks and piping. Cuff flaps blue piped red. Yellow metal buttons. Red epaulettes. Black shako with a red cloth band round the top with a white plume, yellow metal plate and chinscales. In winter, royal blue trousers with red piping. White cross belts supporting pouch and sidearm, the bayonet was carried on the pouch cross belt. Brown cowhide pack and greatcoat strapped to the top in a white bag striped blue. The school at La Flèche had a similar uniform, but with yellow facings, white trousers in summer dress.

Rank distinctions

In full dress officers of the infantry wore a gorget with the Bourbon coat of arms, suspended from buttons that also secured the shoulder straps. Lieutenants wore an epaulette with a silk fringe on the left shoulder and a contre-epaulette, without a fringe on the right. Captains had two fringed epaulettes. A *chef de bataillon* had an epaulette with a bullion fringe on the left shoulder and a contre-epaulette on the right. Colonels and Lieutenant-Colonels had two bullion fringed epaulettes, the colonel with gold, or gilt straps, the lieutenant-colonel with silver straps, or vice versa, depending on the colour of the uniform buttons. In the Guards regiments the epaulettes were silver. NCO ranks were shown above the cuffs, corporals had two wool stripes for tunics with round cuffs, or inverted chevrons for pointed cuffs. In the cavalry regiments the rank of corporal was known as *brigadier*, which has led to much confusion among English speakers. Sergeants had a metallic stripe or chevron in the button colour (*marchal-des-logis* in the mounted troops) and sergeant-majors two metallic stripes. Long service distinctions were shown by wool inverted chevrons on the upper left arm. The senior NCO warrant officer termed *Adjutant* in French wore an officer's uniform and side arm and wore an epaulette and contre epaulette. Corporals and sergeants who held the duty of quartermaster wore, in addition to the cuff stripes, a single stripe on the upper arm.

13

Spanish costumes

The uniforms adopted by the Spanish army after the Napoleonic wars were inspired by French military fashions and by the early 1820s were almost identical. In some illustrations the only way to tell the difference was to look at the colour of the cockade on the shako! Whereas the French Bourbons adopted a white cockade, the Spanish Bourbons stayed with their traditional red cockade. With the revolution the new government decided to change the military cockade to one of blue and red.

By 1823 Spain boasted of at least three armies. Most of the regular troops sided with the Cortes and the liberal movement, while the royalist sympathisers raised volunteer regiments and in the countryside groups of guerrillas fought with the French against the regular troops of the Constitution. The royalist volunteers were armed, equipped and dressed similarly to the French, while the guerrillas forces had no uniform, merely distinguished by some form of coloured patch if anything at all. One illustration shows a guerrilla chief with a French tricolour fixed to his cap. How accurate this is, is questionable, as the regular French troops would look on the tricolour with suspicion!

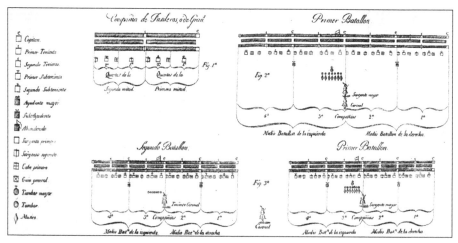

Spanish infantry manual 1820, an infantry regiment of two battalions. (Open source)

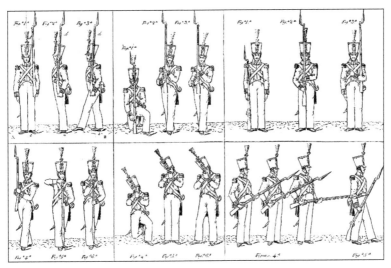

Spanish infantry drill manual. (Open source)

Spanish Guerrilla, from a contemporary print. The brown cloak was a common enough Spanish garment, as are the locally made footwear, but the blue costume is most unusual. He carries an old fashioned flintlock musket with a large knife worn in the waist belt. The red cockade could identify him either as a royalist or a Constitutionalist. (Author's collection)

Spanish *cazador* of a Light infantry battalion, based on Bueno. In this case the cockade has been changed to the Constitutional colours of red and blue, the Bourbon cockade was plain red. (Author's collection)

The regular Spanish infantry was subject to a new uniform regulation issued on the 29 September 1821. They were given a tailcoat of turquoise-blue (a mid-dark blue), single breasted and closed with a row of yellow metal buttons. The collar, round cuffs and turnbacks were red, as was the piping on the front of the coat and on the false pockets on the tails. Pointed cuff flaps in blue with three buttons. The number of the regiment was displayed in yellow on either side of the collar. Red epaulettes for grenadiers. Light grey trousers. Black shako with yellow cloth binding to the top edge and a 'V' shape on either side, yellow metal plate and chinscales. Grenadier companies had a grenade badge in the centre of the pompon and red cords and racquets. All elite companies had white cross belts supporting the pouch and short sabre and bayonet. Grey greatcoat. Personal equipment included a white bread bag carried on a shoulder strap.

Sappers wore a similar blue tail coat with a white apron extending from the chin to the knees, with a white waist belt and a brass buckle. A red badge of crossed axes on the upper left arm, yellow epaulette straps with red fringes and white (some sources show red) aiguillette. White gauntlet gloves. Arms were a musket, sabre and axe. Headgear a fur colpack with a light blue bag edged red, red cords and a red over white plume. A full beard was also obligatory. Drummers wore reversed colours, a red tailcoat with blue collar and cuffs. Yellow epaulettes and cords and racquets on the shako. Grey trousers. The brass drum was carried on a white shoulder belt.

Officers wore a similar uniform with gold shako cords and a white plume. Gilt gorget on service.

The Light infantry wore the same uniform, except that the basic colour of the tail coat was a mid-green. Yellow hunting horn badge on the coat tails and on the collar of the coat. Green or yellow epaulettes and shako cords.

The heavy cavalry regiments wore a yellow coatee with a red collar and red round cuffs and white metal buttons. Grey riding trousers lined with leather and a red stripe down the outside seam. The shoulders were protected with yellow metal shoulder scales and rolls. Brass helmet with brass crest with black horsehair tail and a red plume. Armed with sword and carbine. The shabraque was blue edged white. The light cavalry had a green coatee with red collar and pointed red cuffs. White metal buttons. The same shoulder decorations as the heavy cavalry. The regimental number was shown in yellow on either side of the collar. Riding trousers also as the heavy cavalry. Black shako decorated with yellow cloth tape around the top edge. White cords and racquets and a red plume.

The horse artillery had a blue coatee in a similar cut to the light cavalry, but with a red collar and round cuffs and blue cuff flaps. Red piping on the coatee. Yellow metal buttons and shoulder decorations. Black shako with yellow metal plate and chinscales, red band round the top edge and red cords and pompon. Grenade badge in yellow on either side of the collar.

As soon as the Constitutionalist Government had departed from Madrid a unit of volunteers was raised in the city in support of the royalist cause. It consisted of cavalry and infantry. The cavalry were dressed in a Lancer style uniform, tunic was white with white collar and cuffs both piped with crimson, the plastron was also crimson and the white metal buttons were decorated with white lace. A white fringed epaulette was worn on each shoulder with an aiguillette of mixed white and crimson cord fixed to the front tunic and suspended from the left shoulder. The headgear was a Polish style *chapska* with a black leather body and a crimson coloured square top. A white metal plate on the front, a red cockade held by a gold cord with, above, a white pompon and a white plume. Crimson trousers with double yellow piping on the outside scenes. The curved sabre was carried by silver metal chains fixed to a white waist belt, the belt had a yellow metal clasp. Black shoes with yellow metal spurs. A small pouch was carried on a white leather shoulder strap which was decorated with a yellow metal badge. White gloves with black gauntlet cuffs. The saddlecloth was mid blue with a wide white lace band, black sheepskin.

The infantry followed French fashions, the tailcoat was royal blue closed down the front with yellow metal buttons. The collar was also blue with a scarlet three pointed tab at the front, cuffs also scarlet with blue cuff flaps bearing three small yellow metal buttons. The turn-backs were also red. White cross belts supporting a cartridge pouch and short sword. The grenadiers had a black bearskin cap with a red tassel at the front, but without any metal plates. The plume worn on the left side was red. A patch at the back of the cap was red decorated with a yellow metal bursting grenade badge. The centre companies (*fusileros*) and the light company (*cazadores*) had a French style shako with a yellow metal plate and chin scales, it was decorated with a large red cockade, the centre companies had a white pompon and plume, the light company a

French troops greeted by the citizens of Madrid, contemporary print. (Open source)

yellow pompon and plume. Company distinctions for the grenadiers were red fringed epaulettes, a red sword knot and yellow grenade badges on the turn backs. The light company had yellow epaulettes and a yellow sword knot, fusiliers had white epaulettes and a white sword knot. The elite companies had a particular Spanish distinction of three small yellow lace bars under the cuff with just the points showing. Their Spanish name was 'little sardine'. All wore white trousers of full cut and white gaiters.

The uniforms of the Royalist Spanish troops supplied by the French were quickly adapted to national styles. A light infantry regiment officer is depicted in a blue tailcoat, single breasted and with yellow collar, cuffs and turnbacks. Yellow epaulettes. The shako was decorated with yellow cloth tape round the top, the base and 'V' shapes on each side and a yellow pompon and a large yellow plume, a yellow loop at the front holding a red Bourbon cockade. The coat was worn with several buttons open revealing a white, red striped waistcoat. Round the waist a red sash. The white trousers were patched at the knees, but in tatters at the ankles. Footwear was locally manufactured espadrilles.

The grandly named 'Longa Grenadiers' wore a short jacket and calf length trousers in brown cloth, a red sash and the ubiquitous espadrilles. The headgear a fur cap with a red cloth bag. Arms were a musket and bayonet, a grenadier sabre and knife with a yellow metal handle.

A grenadier of General Longa's corps. (Clerjon de Champagny)

The Lancers of Aranjuez wore a green jacket, with short tails, red collar, plastron and pointed cuffs and red trousers and brown boots. The jacket had white epaulettes and a sash of red and white stripes round the waist. Headgear was a tall conical shako covered in red cloth with a white band round the top, with white cords and flounders and a tall white plume. Arms were a curved sabre carried in a steel scabbard and a wooden lance with steel point and a red over white pennon.

A regiment of light cavalry seems to have been dressed from local stores, a green double-breasted jacket with white metal buttons, with the upper buttons undone to reveal a white shirt with a large collar which overlapped the jacket collar. The jacket had red pointed cuffs and was piped red. Blue-grey trousers lined with brown leather, low shoes with large spurs. Headgear was a black top hat with large brim sporting a large red plume. Arms were a sword in a black leather scabbard with brass fittings and a pair of pistols carried in a red and white striped sash.

Appendix

Who's Who

Álava, Miguel de

1770 to 1843. He has the unusual distinction of having fought at the battle of Trafalgar with the Spanish fleet against Nelson's ships and with the Duke of Wellington at the battle of Waterloo, as Spanish ambassador to the Dutch king. He had become a personal friend of the duke during the Peninsula campaign. On the breaking out of the revolution of 1820, he was chosen by the province of Álava to represent it in the Cortes, where he became conspicuous in the party of the liberals. In 1822 he fought with the militia under Francisco Ballesteros and Pablo Morillo to maintain the authority of the Cortes against the royalists. When the French invested Cadiz, Álava was commissioned by the Cortes to treat with the Duc d'Angoulême, and the negotiations resulted in the restoration of Ferdinand, who pledged himself to a liberal policy. No sooner had he regained power, however, than he ceased to hold himself bound by his promises, and Álava found it necessary to retire first to Gibraltar and then to England where he was given a house on the Duke of Wellington's estate in Hampshire. He later returned to Spain and served the Royal government against the Carlists, even offered the post of Prime Minister in 1835.

Aloysius, Louis, Prince of Hohenlohe-Waldenburg-Bartenstein (German: Ludwig Aloysius Prinz zu Hohenlohe-Waldenburg-Bartenstein)

18 August 1765 to 30 May 1829. A German prince and Marshal of France. He commanded a division of Austrian soldiers in the 1809 and 1814 campaigns during the Napoleonic Wars. Hohenlohe entered French service with the rank of lieutenant general, after the fall of Napoleon and the restoration of the House of Bourbon in 1814. The following year he held the command of a regiment raised by himself, made up of non-French volunteers. The same year he was naturalised a French citizen, upon which he was made a Peer of France. During the Spanish campaign he was given command of the III Corps of the Army of the Pyrenees. In 1827 he was given the distinction of Marshal of France.

Ballesteros, Francisco

1770 to 1832. When the liberal revolution broke out in 1820, he was recalled to Madrid, where on March 7 he surrounded the royal palace and forced King Ferdinand VII of Spain to sign the Spanish Constitution of 1812. He became vice-president of the provisional junta, closing many prisons of the Holy Inquisition and restoring municipal rights.

On 7 July 1822, Ballesteros defeated the Royal Guards, preventing a coup against the Constitution. For this he was named Captain General of Madrid. In 1823 he fought the French invasion under Louis-Antoine, Duke of Angoulême in Navarra and Aragón, but he had to capitulate on August 21, 1823 in Caporla.

On 1 October 1823 Fernando VII started his campaign of repression against all who had supported the constitutional government. Ballesteros fled to Cadiz, where he embarked on a British ship for France. He spent the rest of his life in Paris, where he died on 29 June 1832.

Bordesoulle, Étienne Tardif de Pommeroux de

4 April 1771 to 3 October 1837. On the first return of the Bourbon monarchy, Bordesoulle's noble origins got him an appointment as inspector general of the cavalry in May 1814, knight of the order of Saint Louis on 2 June and grand officer of the *Legion d'Honneur* on 23 August. On Napoleon's return from Elba, Bordesoulle took provisional command of 9 cavalry squadrons of the 2nd military division headed for Châlons on 12 March 1815 and was confirmed in this role by the royal government on 16 March. He followed Louis XVIII of France to Ghent, where he was made chief of staff to the Comte d'Artois (later Charles X of France) on 25 June 1815. He returned to France with the Duke of Berry in July 1815 after the Hundred Days and was made Grand-Cross of the *Légion d'Honneur* by the king on 13 August and appointed to command and reorganise the cavalry of the royal guard on 8 September. Bordesoulle was then elected a centre-right Deputy for Indre in the *Chambre introuvable* (French chamber of Deputies dominated by the ultra-royalist faction) of 1815-1816, and on 12 October was made a member of the commission charged with investigating the conduct of officers during the Hundred Days. On 13 May 1816 he was made a commander of the order of Saint Louis, and exchanged his Napoleonic title of baron for the Bourbon one of comte (count). An honorary aide-de-camp to the comte d'Artois from 2 June 1817 and a member of the committee of the inspectors-general on 25 October, he became a privy councillor of the Duke of Angoulême on 2 July 1820. He was made a Grand-Cross of Saint Louis on 1 May 1821 and was made governor of the *École Polytechnique* on 17 September 1822, all the while retaining his role in the Royal Guard. In 1823, he took part in the Spanish expedition. Summoned on 16 February 1823 to be commander-in-chief of the contingent of the Guards within the Army of the Pyrénées, Bordesoulle organised the bombardment and blockade of Cadiz and was mentioned in despatches on 31 August for his part in the taking of Trocadéro.

Carrel, Jean-Baptiste Nicolas Armand

1800 to 1836. Was born at Rouen. His father was a wealthy merchant, and he received a liberal education at the Lycée Pierre Corneille in Rouen, afterwards attending the military school at St. Cyr. He had a deep admiration for the great generals of Napoleon, and his uncompromising spirit and independent views marked him as a leader. Entered the army as sub-lieutenant. At the outbreak of war with Spain in 1823, Carrel, whose sympathies were with the liberal cause, resigned, and succeeded in escaping to Barcelona. He enrolled in the foreign legion and fought gallantly against his former comrades. The legion was compelled to surrender near Figueras, and Carrel was taken prisoner by his former general, Damas. There was considerable difficulty about the terms of his capitulation, and one council of war condemned Carrel to death. The sentence was not carried out, and he was soon acquitted and freed. Died as a result of a wound received in a duel.

d'Artois, Louis-Antoine, Duke of Angoulême

6 August 1775 to 3 June 1844. He was the eldest son of Charles X king of France and the last to hold the title of Dauphin of France, from 1824 to 1830. He was technically king of France for less than 20 minutes before he abdicated, due to his father's prior abdication during the July Revolution in Paris. After his father's death in 1836 he became the legitimist pretender under the style of Louis XIX. He was probably one of the most exiled royals in history; in 1789 during the Revolution he was exiled from France and went to Turin; in 1795 he returned to lead a rising in the Vendee; left France for Germany and tried to join the Austrian army; had to flee and ended up in Courland, then part of Russia; in 1800 as colonel of a Bavarian cavalry regiment fought at the battle of Hohenlinden; next to Warsaw to escape Napoleon's army; in 1807 exiled to England where he lived in Buckinghamshire until he sailed for Bordeaux in 1814 to again raise the standard of the Bourbon monarchy. At the revolution of 1830 he was forced from France and ended up in Edinburgh at the court of his father, in 1832 the family was offered the use of Prague Castle by the Emperor of Austria. They settled in Graffenberg Castle in Slovenia where he died in1844.

Ferdinand VII, king of Spain

Imprisoned by Napoleon after the abdication of his father. After 1808 the Spanish populace rose against the French invaders in the name of the absent Ferdinand, known as 'the Desired'. In 1812 independent Spaniards adopted the Constitution of Cadiz, but in December 1813 Napoleon released Ferdinand expressly to overthrow it. When Ferdinand returned to Spain in 1814 he was urged by reactionaries to abolish the Cortes of Cadiz and its entire works, which he did almost immediately. He resumed his absolute powers and attempted to recover control of Spanish America, now partly independent. But his ministers could neither reinforce his armies in America nor persuade the British government to collaborate or connive at reconquest. In 1820 a liberal revolution restored the Constitution of 1812, which Ferdinand accepted, but in 1823 Louis XVIII of France sent the Duke of Angoulême at the head of a large army to release Ferdinand from his radical ministers. Ferdinand's new government arrested the radicals or drove them into exile.

Garcés, Colonel

A member of the Cortes and military commander of the Constitutional forces defending the forts on the island of Trocadero.

Guilleminot, Armand

Born 2 March 1774 in Dunkirk and died 14 March 1840 in Baden, Germany. He was a French general of the Revolution and the Empire, a peer of France and ambassador under the Restoration.

In May 1817, he was responsible for setting, together with a German commission and in accordance with the treaties of 1814 and 1815, the line of the French border in the east.

Appointed member of the Defence Committee of the kingdom in 1818, and director of the war ministry in 1822, and helped to reorganise the department. Chief of the General Staff to the Duke of Angoulême in 1823, he directed the Spanish expedition to restore to absolute monarchy the king, Ferdinand VII. Named peer of France and ambassador to Constantinople, he left Spain to take up his post.

Recalled in 1831 by Louis-Philippe I, he became president of the commission to establish the demarcation of the eastern border, and a member of the new Defence Committee which was re-established in 1836.

Lopez-Banos, Miguel

1789 to 1861. Fought against the French during the invasion of 1808, was captured in 1809 and served under King Joseph (Bonaparte). One of the original supporters of the uprising in 1820, active in liberal politics, he served as Minister of War between July 1822 and April 1823. Was given an independent command during the 1823 campaign in the south of Spain. After Ferdinand's return he escaped via Gibraltar to London. Returned to Spain after 1834 where he took several official positions, including governor of Cadiz in 1835.

Louis XVIII, king of France

On 2 May 1814, Louis XVIII officially promised a constitutional monarchy, with a two chamber parliament, religious toleration, and constitutional rights for all citizens. The resulting *Charte Constitutionnelle* was adopted on June 4, 1814. Louis's constitutional experiments were cut short, however, by the return of Napoleon from Elba. After Marshal Michel Ney defected to Napoleon on March 17, 1815, the King fled to Ghent. He did not return until July 8, after Waterloo. Louis XVIII's reign saw France's first experiment in parliamentary government since the Revolution. The King was invested with executive powers and had 'legislative initiative', whereas a largely advisory parliament voted on laws and approved the budget. The legislature, though, had a strong right-wing, royalist majority. Influenced by his favourite, Élie Decazes, who became prime minister in 1819, the King opposed the extremism of the ultras, who were determined to wipe out every vestige of the Revolution, and he dissolved the parliament in September 1816. After 1820, however, the ultras exercised increasing control and thwarted most of Louis's attempts to heal the wounds of the Revolution. At his death he was succeeded by his brother, the comte d'Artois, as Charles X.

Mina, Francisco Espoz y

1781 to 1836. In the campaign of 1813 and 1814 he served with distinction under the Duke of Wellington. After the restoration of Ferdinand VII he fell into disfavour. On 25 and 26 September 1814 he attempted to bring about an uprising at Pamplona in support of the Liberal party, but failed, and went into exile. His political opinions were democratic and radical, and as a non-noble he disliked the "hidalgos" (low-ranking nobles). The Revolution of 1820 brought him back, and he served the Liberal party during the Trienio Liberal in Galicia, Leon and Catalonia. In this last district he made the only vigorous resistance to the French intervention in favour of Ferdinand VII. On 1 November 1823 he was compelled to capitulate, and the French allowed him to escape to England by sea.

Molitor, Gabriel-Jean-Joseph, 1st Count Molitor

7 March 1770 to 28 July 1849, after the abdication of Napoleon, Molitor made his submission to the Bourbons who appointed him Inspector-General of the infantry. Upon the return of the emperor from Elba, Molitor joined him during the Hundred Days, for which he was stripped of his functions after Napoleon's defeat. In 1818, Molitor was restored to grace and in 1823 he commanded the II Corps which was sent to Spain. The same year he was made a Marshal of France as well as a Peer of France. From 1827, he served as secretary to the Chamber of Peers. After the July Revolution, Molitor was allowed to keep all his functions and he later served as Governor of *Les Invalides* and as Grand Chancellor of the *Legion d'Honneur*.

Moncey, Bon-Adrien Jeannot de (or Jannot de Moncey), 1st Duke of Conegliano, 1st Baron of Conegliano

31 July 1754 to 20 April 1842. In 1814 he supported Louis XVIII and was created a Peer of France as Baron of Conegliano (June 1814, confirmed in 1825). He remained neutral during Napoleon's return, the 'Hundred Days', feeling himself bound to Louis XVIII by his engagements as a Peer of France, but after Waterloo he was punished for refusing to take part in the court martial of Marshal Ney by imprisonment and the loss of his marshalate and peerage. The King returned his title of Marshal in 1816, and he re-entered the chamber of peers three years later. He continued his military career: his last active service was as commander of an army corps in Spain in 1823.

Morillo, Pablo, Count of Cartagena and Marquess of La Puerta

1775 to 1837, entered the Spanish military in the regiment of Royal Marines, he was wounded and taken prisoner at the battle of Trafalgar. Fought against the French invasion in 1808. Commanded the Spanish army sent to Central America to retrieve control from the revolutionary forces under Simon Bolivar. This he seemed to achieve and returned to Spain. He supported the 'Liberal' constitution of the Cortes and fought against the French, but with little success. Later supported the French in Galicia. Fled to France after 1823 to escape Ferdinand's retribution.

O'Donnell, Enrique José y Anatar, conde de La Bisbal Count Henry O'Donnell

1769 to 1834. The O'Donnell family left Ireland after the battle of the Boyne, some went to Austria, others to Spain. He fought successfully against the French in Catalonia in 1810, promoted to Field Marshal and awarded the title of Count. He held posts under Ferdinand VII. During the Liberal revolution in 1820 he supported the liberals despite his absolutist convictions, because he was against French intervention. He fled to France where he was interred. After Ferdinand's death he set out for Spain, but died before he could cross the frontier.

Oudinot, Nicolas Charles, 1st Count Oudinot, 1st Duke de Reggio

25 April 1767 in Bar-le-Duc to 13 September 1848 in Paris, was a Marshal of France. He is known to have been wounded 34 times in battle (by artillery fire, bullets [at least 12], sabre cuts and thrusts). His last active service was in the French invasion of Spain in 1823, in which he commanded a corps and was for a time governor of Madrid. He died as governor of the Parisian veterans institution *Les Invalides*.

Ouvrard, Gabriel-Julien

A brilliant, if sometimes unlucky, financier, Ouvrard joined a commercial business house in the last days of the old Bourbon monarchy. His companies won contracts to supply the French navy and the Spanish navy and also the French army of Italy earning enormous sums of money. He spent lavishly on prestigious properties and earned and lost fortunes, even spending time in prison on the orders of Napoleon (when First Consul). He helped the restored French government to pay the indemnity demanded by the Congress of Vienna in 1815 and also to pay for the Allied Army of occupation until its departure in 1818. He organised the commissariat for the army in 1823 which should have made him another fortune, if the government had honoured its obligations to pay the bills. Unfortunately he was made bankrupt, from which he never recovered. He died in London in 1846

Quiroga, General Antonio

1784 to 1841. Began his military career in the Spanish navy as midshipman, later a professor in the Naval College. Liberal army officer, a colonel of the regiment of Catalonia when the revolution broke out in 1820 and the most senior officer to give it his support. He was elected a member of the Cortes. Promoted by the government and later commander of the defenders of Cadiz. He previously held an independent command in northern Spain but his army eventually surrendered to the French at La Coruna. After the defeat of the Constitutionalists he escaped the revenge of the monarchy and lived in exile in London for many years before returning to Spain after the death of Ferdinand.

Riego, Rafael del Riego y Nuñez

9 April 1784 to 7 November 1823. Spanish general and liberal politician. In 1819, the King was forming an army of ten battalions to fight in the Spanish American wars of independence. Riego was given command of a battalion of the Regiment of Asturias. After arriving in Cadiz, together with other liberal officers, he started a mutiny on 1 January 1820, demanding the return of the 1812 Constitution. On 7 April 1823, the French army crossed the borders. Riego took command of the Third Army and resisted the invaders as well as local absolutist groups. On 15 September he was betrayed and taken prisoner on a country estate near the village of Arquillos, in the province of Jaén. He was taken to Madrid. Despite asking for clemency from the King, Riego was found guilty of treason, as he was one of the members of parliament who voted in favour of taking the royal power away from the King. On 7 November 1823, he was hanged at La Cebada Square in Madrid.

Annotated Bibliography

Rather than just give a list of book titles, I have shown sources which are appropriate to each chapter. Also indicated are some details of each source, whether it can be easily obtained and in what language it is written. Fortunately many libraries have, or are in the process of, digitising their holdings and making it generally available to anyone with internet access.

In general, relevant to several chapters

Gallica, the website of the BNF (*Bibliothèque National de France*). Lots of books, maps and a few pictures from the French National collection, material generally in French. <http://gallica.bnf.fr>

Niles' Weekly Register, journal published in Baltimore, USA. The edition for 1823 (volume 24, January to August only) contains a number of 'Foreign News' sections which it gleaned from newspapers arriving principally at New York from England and France. Not just reprinting the news it received, but makes some interesting comments as well. Available through Google Books.

Various websites, from Wikipedia to wargaming, biographical and historical. Search under headings such as: The French invasion of Spain 1823; The Hundred Thousand Sons of St Louis; Battle of the Trocadero, etc.

Chapter 1

Artz, Frederick B., 'Reaction and Revolution 1814-1832', in William L. Langer (ed.), *The Rise of Modern Europe*, Volume XIII (New York and London, 1934). An overview of the Spanish revolution and its effects within the wider political setting of post-Napoleonic Europe.

Ewald, Alexander Charles, *The Last Century of Universal History*, (London: Frederick Warne & Co., 1868). A reference book for those taking the Civil Service examinations in the 1860s.

Fehrenbach, Charles Wentz, 'Moderados and Exaltados: The Liberal Opposition to Ferdinand VII, 1814-1823' *The Hispanic American Historical Review*, Vol. 50, No. 1, 1970, pp. 52–69. <www.jstor.org/stable/2511632>

Hugo, Abel, *The Franco-Spanish War 1823*, translated and edited by Dr. George F. Nafziger (USA, 2009). Translation of the original French work of 1825, with notes and comments by the editor. This book covers the campaign in detail including many of the smaller actions. The author was a royalist sympathiser and the text is heavily biased in favour of the Spanish royalists and of course, the French monarchy. The original work was dedicated to the French king Louis XVIII.

Chapter 2

Detaille, Edouard, *L'Armee Francaise-Types et Uniformes*, English translation of the original French edition published in 1889. This edition published New York, 1992. A mass of information on the history and organisation of the French army from 1790 to 1885. Also includes orders of battle for the various French arms of service sent to Spain in 1823. Beautiful line drawings by Detaille, but no colour plates for the 1820s.

Jenlis, Alain de, 'La Garde Royale de 1815 à 1830', *Uniformes, les armées de l'histoire* magazine, issue 99, December 1986, pp. 5-23. Well illustrated with coloured prints, photographs of uniforms from the French Army Museum in Paris, badges and buttons.

Ministry of War, *Annuaire de l'Etat Militaire de France pour l'annee MDCCCXXIII* (Paris, 1823). Available online through Google Books. The 'Army List' of the French military forces, published annually. Lists all officers of the French army from the minister of war and his staff down to the lowliest sub-lieutenant by regiment and seniority within each regiment. Also gives brief uniform details for each arm of service. In French.

Sicard, M. F., *Histoire des Institutions Militaires des Francais* (Paris, 1834). A series of publications on the development of the French army organisation, uniforms etc. from ancient times to date (i.e. to 1830). In French. Available online.

Pascal, Brahaut & Sicard, *Histoire de L'Armee et de tout les regiments* (Paris, 1864). Volume 4 includes an account of the Spanish campaign. Some colour plates, text in French. Available on *Gallica* website.

Vernet, H. and Lami, E. *Collections raisonnee des uniformes français de 1814 a 1824* (Paris, 1825). Second part of the author's work on the French army from the Revolutionary period, 47 hand coloured plates of all types of uniforms with at least a page of descriptive text (in French). An original copy, now in poor condition, in the National Arts Library in the Victoria & Albert museum.

Chapter 3

Christiansen, E., *The origins of military power in Spain 1800-1854.* (Oxford, 1967).

Clerjon de Champagny, Jules, *Album d'un soldat pendant la campagne d'Espagne en 1823* (Paris, 1829). A series of sketches, both written and illustrated by a lieutenant of the French 13th Chasseurs à Cheval. An eye-witness account of certain scenes and certain people met by the author during the campaign, not a narrative of events. Available on various internet sources. Text in French, illustrations in colour.

Selin, Shannon, is a historical fiction writer living in Vancouver who writes a blog on Napoleon and 19th century history, particularly where it reflects on North America. She has a chapter on the French emigré officer, Charles Lallemand.

Serafín María de Sotto, 3rd Count of Clonard, (known commonly as Conde de Clonard), *História orgánica de las armas de infantería y caballería españolas desde la creación del Ejercito permanente hasta el día* (Madrid, 1851-59). Conde de Clonard was a politician, army officer and historical writer, a descendant of the Irish diaspora of Catholic nobility who left Ireland in the 18th century and in this case settled in Spain. The work is a monumental account of the Spanish army from the formation of regular units until the time of publication (i.e. to the 1850s). It runs to 16 volumes (volume 6 covers the 1820s) and includes black and white and coloured illustrations drawn by Giminez and engraved by Victor Adam, (some of which appear on the internet). Can be viewed electronically at various sites for example on the 'Hathi Trust Digital Library' website. Text in Spanish.

Chapters 4, 5, 6 and 7

Bittard des Portes, René, *Les campagnes de la restauration* (Reprint, Geneva, 1975). Facsimile copy of the original publication of 1899, Alfred Cattier, Tours. Available from the French National Library in digital format. Also available as a British Library Historical Print Edition, facsimile copy of the original in the British Library, comes in a paperback 'print to order' style. Reproduction quality is patchy, but readable. Based upon official sources and documents, lots of detail, orders of battle. As well as the Spanish campaign also includes French military expeditions to Greece, Madagascar and the initial invasion of North Africa in 1830. Includes orders of battle and biographies of many of the French senior officers. Text in French.

Guillemard, Robert, *Adventures of a French Sergeant, during his campaigns in Italy, Spain, Germany etc. from 1803 to 1823* (London, 1826). The author fought over much of Europe in Napoleon's army and his last campaign was in Spain in 1823, where he was captured almost at the beginning of hostilities. His captors were Italian and French liberals fighting for the Spanish, which perhaps explains how he managed to survive to write his memoirs.

Hugo, Abel, *France militaire. Histoire des armées françaises de terre et de mer* (Paris, 1832). A history of French military campaigns, volume five covers the period 1812 to 1837. In French, with a number of line drawings of uniforms, battle scenes and personalities.

Hugo, Abel, *The Franco-Spanish War 1823* (Paris, 1824). Same as above.

Faits d'Armes de l'Armee francaise en Espagne dédiés à l'armée des Pyrénées sous les ordres de son Altesse Royale Mgr. le duc'Angoulême, (Paris, 1824). Available in digital format from the Basque digital library <http://www.liburuklik.euskadi.net/handle/10771/12303> Original in French. An odd format, with double page spreads set out by day and month, actions, French officers, Spanish commanders and lastly a description of the action naming individuals who had performed some feat of bravery. Includes a detailed French Order of Battle (down to battalion level). As can be seen from the printing details, it was written to publicise the glorious feats of arms of the royal French army.

The Edinburgh Annual Register for 1823, Vol 16 Parts I, II & III (London, 1824). Format similar to below, but content is different.

The New Annual Register for the Year 1823 (London, 1824). Review of the year, political and social, with chapters on the history of Europe.

United Services Magazine, 1832, Vol. 10, Part 3 (London, 1832). Articles entitled 'Sketches of the war of the French in Spain in the year 1823'. The author describes himself as 'a Royalist', which tells you all you need to know. However it contains many small interesting details. In English.

Victoires, conquêtes, désastres, revers et guerres civiles des Français (Paris, 1823). Volume 28 in the series is entitled *Guerre d'Espagne de 1823*. A military, i.e. less politically motivated account of the campaign with what seems like realistic orders of battle of the French army and detailed maps of Madrid, Catalonia and Cadiz. Text in French. Available from the French National Library in digital format.

Chapter 8

Steele, Thomas, *Notes of the war in Spain: Detailing Occurrences Military and Political in Galicia, and at Gibraltar and Cadiz* (London, 1824). Steele belonged to the 'Spanish Committee' in London and took supplies to Corunna to hand over to Sir Robert Wilson and then accompanied him to Cadiz and later escaped to Gibraltar. Interviews with many of the leading liberal Spanish generals. Available online.

Chapter 10

Chasseriau, F. *Precis Historique de la Marine Francaise* (Paris, 1845). Similar list to that in the title below, but the chapter on the Spanish campaign contains copies of the French admiral's dispatches detailing the actions and recommending officers and sailors for awards. In French. Available online.

Faits d'Armes de l'Armee francaise en Espagne dédiés à l'armée des Pyrénées sous les ordres de son Altesse Royale Mgr. le duc'Angoulême, (Paris, 1824). Contains the names of all French ships, by type, where they were stationed during the campaign and their commanders.

Chapter 12

Aubry, Charles, *Collection des uniformes de l'Armee française presentee au Roi par S.E.M. le Marechal Duc de Bellune, Ministre de la Guerre* (Paris, 1823). Album of prints of the French army in the uniforms worn in 1822/1823, good coverage of Guard units. No text.

Funken, L. & F., *L'uniforme et les arms des soldats du XIX siecle*, vol. 1 (Belgium, 1981) In French, very well illustrated in full colour throughout.

Joly, Colonel, *Uniformes des troupes Francais sous la Restauration 1814-1830*, no place, no date. An album of original watercolours painted by Colonel Joly held in the French National Library, 67 plates beautifully executed showing all branches of the French army, Guards and Line from the First Restoration of the Bourbons to the deposition of Charles the Tenth. No text. See: <http://catalogue.bnf.fr/ark:/12148/cb403564190>

Malibran, H., *Album du Guide a l'usage des artistes et des costumiers*, (Krefeld, 1972). Originally published in Paris in 1907, covers the period 1780 to 1848, a reference for artists etc., in two volumes, a text volume of 941 pages covering all formations of the French army with detailed descriptions of all aspects of uniform from hats to shoes! Also weapons, signal instruments, badges and buttons. The second volume consists of over 200 plates of line drawings with between two and 15 drawings on each plate. In French.

Martin, Yves. A French collector with a vast library of books on uniforms, photographic copies from public and private sources.

Moltzheim, Auguste de, *L'Armee Francaise sous la Restauration 1814-1830* (Reprint, Nantes, 2005). Magnificent series of over 600 colour plates painted by de Moltzheim between 1875 and still unfinished at his death in 1881. No text.

Rousselot, Lucien, *La Garde Royale, 1814-1830*. Series of paintings by Rousselot prepared for a private client and now housed in a museum in Nancy, France. Hand written captions to accompany the 28 watercolour paintings.

Vernet, H. and Lami, E. *Collections raisonnee des uniformes français de 1814 a 1824.* (See above)

Chapter 13

Bueno, J. M. *Soldados de Espana* (Madrid, 1998). Magnificent work by the celebrated Spanish military artist José María Bueno Carrera. The Spanish armed forces from the mid-1400s to the 1990s. In Spanish, but with hundreds of thumbnail illustrations of uniforms in colour.

Jou, Francesc Riart and Cardona F. Xavier Hernandez, *Soldats, guerrers I combatents dels paisos Catalans* (Barcelona, 2014). Uniforms of troops raised, or engaged in the Catalonian region from ancient to modern times, several pages on the Barcelona militia in the 1820s. Illustrations in colour, text in Catalan.

Chapter 14

Mainly from open source websites, search by name. In various languages, English, French and Spanish.

Index

PEOPLE

PLACES

MILITARY FORMATIONS & UNITS

MISCELLANEOUS

Milton Keynes UK
Ingram Content Group UK Ltd.
UKHW021811181023
430873UK00006B/111